# Virginia Woolf at Home

# Virginia Woolf at Home

*Hilary Macaskill*

Pimpernel Press Ltd
www.pimpernelpress.com

Pimpernel Press Limited
www.pimpernelpress.com

Virginia Woolf at Home
Copyright © Pimpernel Press Limited 2019
Text © Hilary Macaskill 2019
Photographs © as credited on page 208

Designed by Becky Clarke

Hilary Macaskill has asserted her right to be identified as the author of this book in accordance with the Copyright, Designs and Patents Act 1988.

All rights reserved. No part of this publication may be reproduced, stored in a retrieval system or transmitted, in any form, or by any means, electronic, mechanical, photocopying, recording or otherwise, without prior permission in writing from the publisher or a licence permitting restricted copying. In the United Kingdom such licences are issued by the Copyright Licensing Agency, Barnard's Inn, 86 Fetter Lane, London EC4A 1EN.

A catalogue record for this book is available from the British Library.

Typeset in Adobe Caslon

ISBN 978-1-910258-69-9

Printed and bound in China

9 8 7 6 5 4 3 2 1

PAGE 2 Virginia Stephen, aged 20. Studio portrait by George Charles Beresford.
ABOVE The faraway view of Godrevy lighthouse that was so important in Virginia's childhood summers at Talland House, St Ives, and which inspired *To the Lighthouse*.

# Contents

7    Foreword by Cecil Woolf

8    The Ideal Childhood – Talland House
*'The best beginning to life conceivable'*

28    A Victorian Home – 22 Hyde Park Gate
*'A complete model of Victorian society'*

44    'The Light and the Air' – Bloomsbury
*'Home at last to our native Bloomsbury'*

72    Marriage and Partnership – Hogarth House
*'This beautiful and loveable house'*

98    A Haunted House – Asheham House
*'The flawless beauty of Asheham'*

112    London Renewed – 52 Tavistock Square
*'To walk alone through London is the greatest rest'*

142    A House of One's Own – Monk's House
*'There's nothing I enjoy more than looking for houses'*

178    The Legacy
*'What cuts the deepest channels in our lives are the different houses in which we live'*

198    Timeline of Houses
199    Timeline of Books
200    Bibliography
202    Index
207    Acknowledgments
208    Picture Credits

Leonard and Virginia with Sally, their black-and-white spaniel, at 52 Tavistock Square in 1939.

# Foreword

## by Cecil Woolf

It has been an illuminating experience to be transported back, in the pages that follow, to my boyhood, when my uncle and aunt, Leonard and Virginia, visited my home in Buckinghamshire and I stayed from time to time with them at 52 Tavistock Square, or in the country at Monk's House.

That was some eighty years ago and it never occurred to me that half a century on Virginia would be the literary megastar every detail of whose life and work would be studied and analysed across the world, still less that I should later become the last person alive who actually knew Virginia.

'What was she like?' I'm often asked. As Virginia herself knew, it's a difficult question. In her essay on Dr Johnson's friend Mrs Thrale (it was her last essay), she writes that just when we think we have caught the bird, she flutters off. My own child's-eye memory was that she was endlessly curious about the world and people around her. Henry James's advice to the aspiring novelist was 'Observe constantly'. Virginia was a consummate observer. She was many other things beside, but I must not omit something that is frequently forgotten, she was conspicuously humorous and great fun to be with. Leonard told me that during the First World War, when he and Virginia and the staff of their Richmond house took refuge at night from enemy bombing, Virginia made the servants laugh so much, he was obliged to complain that he was unable to sleep.

Now there is such interest in all aspects of her life and times – and her homes. After three decades in publishing, I began publishing a number of monographs in the Bloomsbury Heritage series. The first title was juvenilia, written by Virginia at the age of 10 or 12, called *A Cockney's Farming Experiences*. Since then, as well as unpublished texts by Bloomsbury friends, like Clive Bell, E.M. Forster and Lytton Strachey, there have been pamphlets on her houses – Monk's House, Talland House, Asheham, as well as 52 Tavistock Square, the home of the Woolfs' publishing company. The most recent is *The Other Boy at Hogarth Press*, which is of my memories of the Press.

I was inspired to start the series after I published the first-ever Bloomsbury title on my list, Jean Moorcroft Wilson's classic and widely acclaimed *Virginia Woolf, Life and London: a Biography of Place*. Hilary Macaskill's excellent book will, no doubt, take its place on the same shelf.

# The Ideal Childhood – Talland House

## *'The best beginning to life conceivable'*

---

It was in Cornwall at Talland House in St Ives, the holiday home of the Stephen family, where the foundations of Virginia Woolf's life – and distinctive style of writing – were laid. Born Adeline Virginia Stephen (though her first name was never used) on 25 January 1882, she was a baby of six months when first taken with her family to Cornwall – she spent her first thirteen summers there. Although Virginia was born in London, it was St Ives, where she spent two to three months each year, that was the more significant.

Talland House remained a fundamental part of her consciousness all her life as she sought to reproduce the sense of place remembered so clearly from her childhood here. Transmuting her memories into fiction was one of the distinctive aims that she had in her later life as a writer, as she delved into the recesses of her memory, sifting through images, tweaking and reworking the recalled sensations.

In her autobiographical 'Sketch of the Past', begun in late 1939, eighteen months before she died, she recreated her experience of lying in bed 'half asleep, half awake' in the nursery at Talland House and 'hearing the waves breaking, one, two, one two, and sending a splash of water over the beach; and then breaking, one, two, one, two, behind a yellow blind.' The light, the sound of the sea and of the noise of the blind 'drawing its little acorn across the floor' as the wind blew through the open window led to her feeling that 'it is almost impossible that I should be here; of feeling the purest ecstasy I can conceive.'

Julia Stephen with Virginia, Vanessa and Thoby at Talland House in St Ives, bought by Leslie Stephen in 1882.

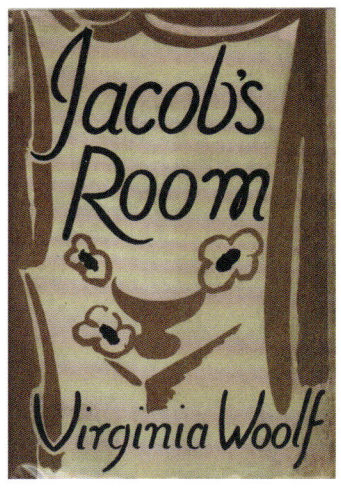 

*Jacob's Room*, the first of Virginia's novels to be inspired by St Ives, and *To the Lighthouse*, with its echoes of Talland House, represent the long collaboration with Vanessa, who designed the covers.

This acute sensibility is reflected throughout her fiction in vivid images that echo her experiences in all her novels, though the one that most closely matched life at Talland House was *To the Lighthouse,* written in 1926 when she was in her mid-forties. The absorbed sights and sounds around her were resurrected for her third novel *Jacob's Room,* published in 1922. In an early draft, later discarded, she writes of Jacob taking a sheep's jawbone that he had found on the beach to bed. The dreamy, half-awake, half-sleeping senses of the child are pricked through by the clear recollections of the nursery there:

*'The blind was thin yellow, curved out, for the nursery window was open. It curved fuller, & then was sucked in. At the same time the sea made that dull noise; then the water was drawn back; then it made the dull noise again. . . The little trailing noise that the knob on the blind cord made as it was drawn along the floor made him open his eyes. The purple petals were falling from the flower on the chest-of-drawers . . .'*

In *The Waves*, published nearly a decade later in 1931, the memories are mined again but in a more impressionistic vein. The constant susurration of the sea, the sounds and scenes punctuating the stages of life of the six characters from childhood onwards, stem from the experience of the infant Virginia, in her nursery watching the light on the ceiling, or playing on the beach and hearing the waves breaking on the sand.

Talland House had been discovered by her father, Leslie Stephen, in 1881 on one of his habitual walking tours of Cornwall. Leslie, author and critic, was, at the time of Virginia's birth in 1882, editor of *The Cornhill Magazine*, a literary periodical founded by the publisher George Smith, and at the height of his professional powers. That same year, he would add to his already extensive reputation by moving to take on the editorship of the *Dictionary of National Biography*, a post shared with Smith, its founder. Its gargantuan aim was to incorporate biographical essays on the distinguished people of Britain from early times. This was to be the start of a period of extremely hard work that took its toll on the family too. But Talland House proved its worth. 'We have made a great hit in taking the house, which is perfect for our requirements,' he wrote to Smith. 'I shall, I hope, come back ready to write and edit biographies by the dozen.' As indeed he did.

As a young man, Leslie had been a pioneering mountaineer; the first to record the sport of sea-cliff climbing, and president of the Alpine Club. For four years from 1868, he had been editor of *Alpine Journal*. Virginia remembered alpenstocks in her nursery and a map of the Alps showing every peak her father had climbed. Now that he could no longer indulge his long-held passion for the Alps, he had found Cornwall to be 'a pleasing substitute', as he wrote to his friend Charles Norton, American academic and editor. 'The scenery is very characteristic and grand, with a sense of oceanic mystery. That is not, according to me, quite equal to the mountains: but it is the next thing to it; and for purposes of sleepy indolence it is perhaps even better. . .'

Sleepy indolence was not the real reason for his new attachment (nor indeed was such a state of mind likely for a man of his energy): his Cornwall walking tours were an escape from the hectic household he left behind in London at 22 Hyde Park Gate in Kensington, in which two bereaved families had merged.

Leslie's first wife, Harriet (known as Minny), was the younger daughter of the novelist William Makepeace Thackeray. They had married in 1867 and first lived at 16 Onslow Gardens in Kensington with Minny's older sister, Anny, a novelist, before they moved, with their daughter Laura, to 8 Southwell Gardens. After Minny's sudden death in 1875, Leslie, together with Laura and Anny, moved to 11 (later renumbered as 24) Hyde Park Gate, where they already knew one of the neighbours, Julia Duckworth, widowed after four years of marriage and mother of three children.

Leslie came to rely on Julia more and more for advice concerning Laura, who, it had become apparent, was backward. Indeed, after Anny's marriage and departure from the house, he made Julia a guardian of Laura. It was not long before Leslie declared himself to be in love with Julia; they married in 1878, and Leslie moved into 13 Hyde Park Gate (renumbered as 22 six years later), the home Julia shared with George, Stella and Gerald – who were then aged ten, nine and eight.

Further Stephen children followed fast: Vanessa was born the following year, followed by Thoby in 1880 and, on 25 January 1882, Virginia. The youngest child, Adrian, was born in 1884. So Leslie's long walks in Cornwall were a welcome release from such a large family. The railway had arrived at St Ives in 1877, four years before his discovery of Talland House, increasing visitors and its population of artists but making his trips easier.

This hilly town of cobbled streets, steep flights of steps and alleyways, is now known for its artistic connections, its fishing-net lofts converted into studios: the sculptor Barbara Hepworth's home is open to visitors, the Tate Gallery has

# THE IDEAL CHILDHOOD – TALLAND HOUSE

In Virginia's day the harbour at St Ives was busy with fishing boats: fishing was the main industry.

had an outpost here since 1993, with a new extension opened in 2017, displaying work by locals like Patrick Heron, Ben Nicholson and Alfred Wallis. But in the late nineteenth century St Ives was primarily a fishing town. It was, as Virginia later described it, 'a steep, windy, noisy, fishy, vociferous, narrow-streeted town the colour of a mussel or a limpet; like a bunch of rough shellfish, oysters or mussels, all crowded together.'

Leslie was charmed by the town and on one of his walks, he found Talland House. 'Did I tell you,' he told Charles Norton, 'that I have bought a little house at St Ives, down at the very toe-nail of England? . . . The children will be able to run

Talland House, the Stephens' summer home for thirteen years, was surrounded by escallonia hedges that divided the grounds into a series of garden 'rooms'.

Even on holiday at Talland House, the Stephen children were given lessons in the dining room. (From left) Thoby, Vanessa, Virginia, Julia and Adrian.

# THE IDEAL CHILDHOOD – TALLAND HOUSE

Godrevy lighthouse, built in 1859, provided the inspiration for one of Virginia's best-known books, *To the Lighthouse*.

straight out of the house to a lovely bit of sand and have good air and quiet.'

It was actually a large house – a square white Regency villa, with elegant windows and balconies, and walls starred with purple-streaked passion flowers. He bought the lease of the house, part of the Tregenna Castle Estate, which was owned by the Great Western Railway Company, from a Mr Bolitho. (In a strange coincidence, Bolitho's great-nephew, Richard Kennedy, many years later worked at the Hogarth Press, set up by Virginia and Leonard Woolf: many more years later he produced a memoir of that time, *A Boy at the Hogarth Press*.)

The downstairs rooms were spacious (the sitting room had a small room at the back used as a den by Leslie when he had had enough of guests). The dining room

Talland House is little changed in appearance from Virginia's day (a side extension was added in the early 1900s), but most of the garden has been lost to modern flats and villas.

was also where the children had lessons during their long summers, though this must have been endlessly distracting as it had French windows leading out to the garden, with a huge view of the sea, just as in *To the Lighthouse* – Virginia wrote in 'A Sketch of the Past' of looking 'over the lesson book and seeing the lights changing on the waves'. A staircase led to the flat roof surrounded by railings and its unsurpassable view of St Ives Bay and Godrevy lighthouse. On a clear day it was possible, so Leslie Stephen boasted, to see thirty miles of coast.

Apart from the view, the best thing was the garden, 'an acre or two, all up and down hill, with quaint little terraces divided by hedges'. When trying to entice a family friend to visit he described it as a 'little garden, which is not much to boast of'. It was actually rather large (two or three acres, Virginia casually remembered). Steps from the road led up to the garden gate, which had a distinctive clicking sound that she remembered always. A stream ran randomly down the hill, eventually ending in a pool created by Mr Lobb the caretaker, who also had made

The steps up to the garden gate at Talland House.

a bench for Julia under a bower of roses, and, in their absence, tended the grape house and dug up the potatoes.

The grounds, as Leslie described to a friend, consisted of 'a dozen little gardens each full of romance for the children – lawns surrounded by flowering hedges, and intricate thickets of gooseberries and currants, and remote nooks of potatoes and peas, and high banks down which you can slide in a sitting posture, and corners in which one can come upon unexpected poppies, altogether a pocket-paradise.'

Each of the different areas, mainly divided by escallonia bushes, was named: the fountain, the cricket lawn, the kitchen garden, the big tree, coffee corner. The Lookout was a grassy mound that rose over the garden wall, a good vantage point to see the railway line and the station. When visitors were expected, the children would watch for the signal to go down and then alert the grown-ups, who would go down to greet the train. It was also the spot for a perfect view of St Ives Bay. There was always activity there: fishing boats, tramp steamers, sailing out or steaming in. In early autumn the pilchard boats were hauled down to the edge of the water, ready for the call from the Huer, the watchman in his little white watch house up on the cliff, looking out for the shoals. In their time as children that call never came, but there was always the excited anticipation.

The main focus of the bay for the family was the Godrevy lighthouse. Built in 1859 to mark dangerous rocks, the Nine Maidens, it was distant but – then – almost always visible from windows, garden and the rooftop, and its comforting presence at night, with its regular and dependable sweep of amber light, was a

In the distance, Godrevy lighthouse with, in the foreground, the lighthouse added at the end of the pier in 1890.

companion. The significance and omnipresence of the lighthouse in *To the Lighthouse* echoed the importance of it in the young Virginia's life as she lay in bed at night.

Talland House was a joyful, chaotic muddle of a home, a place of comfort and happiness. It was shabby, very like the sitting room in *To the Lighthouse* in which Mrs Ramsay glances round at the trailing curtains and beaten-up armchairs – but that was part of its appeal, especially to children. For them this was a paradise – life was much more casual and relaxed. The children swam from nearby Porthminster Beach, changing in one of the bathing tents for hire. They'd walk down the steep path to the beach, pausing to look at the gardens that were below the level of the road, the apples on the trees that were at head height.

Though they were, in the main, summer visitors, Leslie and Julia involved themselves in St Ives affairs. Both joined the St Ives Arts Club, and through Julia's involvement in the community, they were both well known. Leslie became vice-president of the swimming and sailing association: an annual treat was the St Ives Regatta, with its bands and bunting, a crowd of little boats racing among the floating flags.

Leslie continued with his dictionary; Julia would set out most days to visit the poor of St Ives and to tend to the sick – this solicitude was carried over from her work in London, where she visited hospitals and slums: she supported the

## THE IDEAL CHILDHOOD – TALLAND HOUSE

St Ives Bay painted by Thomas Millie Dow, the Scottish artist who bought Talland House from Leslie Stephen in 1895.

Julia and Leslie Stephen reading at Talland House, with Virginia in the background, in 1893.

work of the social reformer Octavia Hill in her efforts to promote better housing for the poor, and brought up her older daughter Stella to follow in her footsteps. Julia was constantly altruistic, perhaps at the expense of her brood of children.

Visitors came and went – relatives, artists (John Everett Millais, Edward Burne-Jones and George Frederic Watts) and Leslie's eminent friends, many of whom stayed in the seemingly elastic-sided home. The author Henry James was among those who preferred the relative luxury of nearby Tregenna Castle Hotel. The poet George Meredith lived in St Ives and would come into the Talland House garden to read poetry to Julia's mother. A favourite guest was James Lowell, an American academic and politician, and Virginia's godfather (notwithstanding that there was no God in the Stephen family's life); he caused envy among her siblings when he gave her a caged bird.

## THE IDEAL CHILDHOOD – TALLAND HOUSE

Summer at St Ives was, without doubt, the 'best beginning to life conceivable'. It began at Paddington Station in London on the Great Western Railway – a journey that took all day and involved changing on to the small branch line at St Erth, four miles from St Ives. It must have been a hectically exciting changeover, with the adults scrambling children (in early years including a baby or a toddler) and all the luggage containing everything needed for their summer on to the small train to St Ives. The fifteen-minute ride along the coast, past the long, sandy beaches and that thrilling first glimpse of the lighthouse, ended close to their home. By then it was almost dusk. Virginia recalled the excitement of arrival in the dark, the stir of going up to bed in a different nursery – and one that shared a balcony with her parents' bedroom. The balcony was partitioned, but seeing her mother come out in a white dressing gown must have been a moment of unusual intimacy for a child whose London nursery was two floors away from her parents' bedroom. It was a signal of a completely different life.

Just as enticing was the location of the nursery over the kitchen, which – again unlike London – was not in the basement, and which must have been a treat in itself for the cook Sophie Farrell, who was part of the entourage. The children upstairs would, on occasion, let down a basket on a piece of string to the kitchen window. If Sophie were in a good mood, she would put some scraps from the grown-ups' dinner in it for them to haul up in glee. If she weren't, she would cut the string. The informality of this ad hoc arrangement, so different from their customary routine, was exhilarating.

Released from the regime of Hyde Park Gate, where chaperones were required for excursions into town, they were allowed to roam. There was so much more freedom here. This was a place where imagination could take flight. Inevitably, in this consciously literary and imaginative family, there were stories shared by the children – about, for example, the spirits Beccage and Hollywinks, who lived in the rubbish heap and exited through a gap in the escallonia hedge.

The Stephen children formed a tight unit, the half-siblings a more shadowy presence in reminiscences. They were a decade or more older; Gerald and George, for the latter Talland House years, were not even there much of the time, being either at university or working. They do not feature a great deal in either Virginia's or Vanessa's memories of those days at Talland House. Except, that is, for one shattering incident that Virginia did not talk about until the end of her life, a moment of utter shame when she was very young and Gerald, a lusty teenage boy, lifted her up on to a ledge in the hall outside the dining room and, putting his hand under her clothes, proceeded to explore her body. In 1939, two years before her death, she could still recall the feelings of dislike, intense shame and powerlessness, an event that must have had implications ever more. It is all the more shocking for its intrusion into what was otherwise an idyllic part of childhood.

But it is the idyllic that is in the forefront of the memories, and the background is the garden. Stella, inspired by their great-aunt, the renowned photographer Julia Margaret Cameron (whose portraits of Julia Stephen as a young woman were famous), had a camera, so the photographs of the children at play are captured forever. There was a lot of cricket: George patiently taught his young half-siblings the principles of the game. Virginia was particularly good – her brothers called her the demon bowler. It was here at the cricket lawn, when she was eleven, that she first met Rupert Brooke – then just six years old – with his brother Dick: their family was on holiday too.

Stella's diary of 1893, when she was twenty-five, recounts a fairly typical day where Vanessa (then fifteen) was painting in the garden alongside Stella, while Virginia and her brothers went fishing and 'Father botanised'. Virginia later decided that she didn't like fishing. She did have a momentary glimpse of the thrill of catching fish, but she knew – though he had not forbidden it – Leslie disapproved of it and that was enough to deter her: his influence was strong all her life.

There was always a great deal of walking. Every afternoon Leslie would demand company, which, in effect, meant a three-line whip, turning into what Virginia called a penance. There was a regular walk around Fairyland, a wood behind granite walls, tufted with moss and flowers, along which the children walked, gazing down to the giant ferns between the oak trees. They might go to the Knills monument, the fifty-foot pyramid at the top of Worvas Hill, which commemorates a former Lord Mayor of St Ives – who erected it in his lifetime, intending it to be his mausoleum, though in fact he died elsewhere and it isn't. But every five

# THE IDEAL CHILDHOOD – TALLAND HOUSE

Cricket was a favourite pastime at Talland House. (Right) Virginia with Vanessa batting. (Below) A younger Virginia, and Adrian batting.

years there is a ceremony of remembrance of this man who so loved St Ives, with a procession and dancing by 'ten maids under ten'.

On Sunday, there was almost always a hike to the ancient hill fort on Trencrom Hill with its granite outcrops, now in the care of the National Trust. From its summit are views to the east of St Ives Bay and to the west St Michael's Mount – a spot to see the sun rise and set. On a return visit to Trick Robin, as they used to call it, by the four Stephen siblings years later, Virginia was gratified to find that they knew every step of the way.

But above all, it was the sea that figured so largely in Virginia's sense of the place, and more than two decades later, the Godrevy lighthouse had the starring role in *To the Lighthouse*, Virginia's novel that – though set in Skye – was actually about her St Ives life (and indeed, incongruously, moved the habitat and birds of Cornwall to Skye). One edition of *Hyde Park Gate News*, the occasional journal produced by the Stephen children, reported that 'Master Adrian' (then nine) was 'much disappointed' at not being allowed to join the trip to the lighthouse. The opening scene of the book replicates that occasion where James, his mother's favourite (just as Adrian was Julia's) cannot make the longed-for trip. Many real-life episodes are echoed here. A guest at Talland House lost her brooch on the beach, and the town crier broadcast this. Did she get it back? We don't know. Just as we don't know if Minta retrieved the brooch of pearls that she lost on the Skye beach that so resembled the beach of St Ives.

In 1895, when Virginia was thirteen, the summers full of freedom and fresh air – in such stark contrast to life at 22 Hyde Park Gate – came to an end when her mother died. But St Ives remained with her all her life as a yardstick for happiness. In June 1923, for example, as she wrote in her diary, she had a familiar feeling of suppressed excitement about the 'poetry of existence that overcomes me. Often it is connected with the sea and St Ives.'

In years to come there would be many visits to Cornwall. Between 1908 and 1910, Virginia went there six times: not insignificantly perhaps, these were in the two years after Vanessa's marriage when she felt abandoned. But the first return was with her three siblings in 1905 when together they returned to St Ives in a mission to revisit their childhood. They stayed from August until October.

# THE IDEAL CHILDHOOD – TALLAND HOUSE

Trencrom Hill, a favourite destination of the Stephen family's walks.

They made the same excursions, trod the same walks, took boat trips and visited the woman who took in their washing, the farmer's daughter who used to bring chickens and helped in the house, and the old man who kept the bathing tents. They even went into Talland House, invited to tea by the new owners, Thomas and Florence Millie Dow, 'a delightful pair of artists, with a family the age we used to be.'

But what permeated her consciousness until the end of her life was their first visit to see Talland House at dusk on the day they arrived, as she recounted in 'A Sketch of the Past'. 'We passed through the gate, groped stealthily but with sure feet up the carriage drive, mounted the little flight of rough steps, & peered through a chink in the escallonia hedge.' They gazed up at the lighted windows, at the terrace with the stone urns, feeling as though they left it just that morning. 'We hung there like ghosts in the shade of the hedge, & at the sound of footsteps we turned away.'

# A Victorian Home – 22 Hyde Park Gate

## *'A complete model of Victorian society'*

The contrast between the airiness, freedom and light of Talland House and 22 Hyde Park Gate could not have been more extreme. The Stephens' London home was solidly Victorian. It was imposing, hemmed in by neighbouring houses and embodying constraint. The house was dark and the street was narrow. It was also immensely fashionable.

Hyde Park Gate is a cul-de-sac of houses not far from the Royal Albert Hall and opposite Kensington Gardens. Leslie Stephen described it as 'a little backwater of a street', though it can hardly be called that now. One mansion has a pavement patrol of black-suited security men; even a four-bedroom flat fetches over five million pounds. In fact, it may never have merited Leslie Stephen's description, even at the start of its existence.

It was the creation of Joshua Flesher Hanson, a schoolmaster turned developer. His first project was Regency Square in Brighton, begun in 1818, but in the 1820s he moved to Kensington, where he first established Campden Hill Square and then, in 1833, turned to this patch of land, a field which provided grazing for donkeys and had been owned until his death two years earlier by the Swiss-born Durs Egg of Pall Mall, innovative gunmaker to George IV.

The first houses on the site – a clutch of three on the west side – were ready for occupation by 1836. Thereafter, building was intermittent. Hanson gave leases to builders, and the block from 19 to 24 was built in 1843, in three sets of semi-

22 Hyde Park Gate, where Virginia was born.

detached houses, the year Hanson himself moved in to Hyde Park Gate, though his home has now been replaced by a block of flats, Chancellor's House.

It became an elite road: even in the nineteenth century several of the occupants in Hyde Park Gate, aptly enough, had entries in the *Dictionary of National Biography*. Other authors have also lived here, such as Enid Bagnold (whom Virginia met in later life), the sculptor Jacob Epstein lived at 18; and it was the home of many MPs over the years, including Winston Churchill, who lived (and died) here at 28, almost opposite the Stephen family home. Churchill also owned the next-door house, 27, using it for his offices. This was originally the home of Mrs Redgrave, whom Virginia could so easily see from her night nursery washing her neck before she went to bed, a potent image that was reproduced in *Mrs Dalloway*, where Clarissa looks out of her window and sees an old woman in the house opposite.

It's possible that the widowed Leslie's move to this road in 1876 with his daughter and sister-in-law Anny was made on information from Julia Duckworth, who lived in Hyde Park Gate. She was a friend of Anny's, and came to know Leslie and Minny well through that friendship – though, in fact, Leslie had first encountered Julia in 1866, when she was twenty years old and then Julia Jackson, whose mother was one of the seven Pattle sisters who held much sway in the society of their day. One aunt was the photographer Julia Margaret Cameron. Another aunt, Sarah Prinsep, held a celebrated salon at Little Holland House in Kensington. On Sunday afternoons, politicians such as William Gladstone and Benjamin Disraeli mingled with authors William Thackeray, Thomas Carlyle and Alfred Tennyson, as well as Pre-Raphaelite artists such as Dante Gabriel Rossetti and William Holman Hunt (for some of whom Julia modelled). Leslie remembered the house as a quaint old-fashioned building like a rambling farmhouse with a large garden, but, in a fit of early town planning, it was demolished in 1874 in favour of a road (Melbury Road). Virginia remembered being taken to the site by her mother on a nostalgic visit; for Julia too the sense of place was important.

Julia had visited Leslie and Minny, who was pregnant, on the evening of 27 November 1875 at their home in Southwell Gardens. According to Leslie's account in his *Mausoleum Book*, she had felt that she was intruding on their happiness,

# A VICTORIAN HOME – 22 HYDE PARK GATE

22 Hyde Park Gate has the distinction of being the only house in London to have three plaques – for Leslie, Vanessa and Virginia.

Julia Stephen, in a famous portrait by her aunt, pioneering photographer Julia Margaret Cameron.

contrasting it with her own solitary state as a young widow, and she had not stayed long. The very next day Minny died of puerperal eclampsia. It was Leslie's birthday. He never celebrated his birthday again.

Afterwards, as near neighbours in Hyde Park Gate, Julia provided sympathetic support. Anny's subsequent departure from the household after her marriage in 1877 to her cousin Richmond Ritchie (a late match: she was aged forty and he was twenty-three) left Leslie, a still-grieving widower, alone with his six-year-old daughter, so it was natural that he turned even more to Julia. It seemed inevitable that he should fall in love with this beautiful and thoughtful woman. In 1878 they married, and Leslie and Laura moved into Julia's home at 13 (later 22) Hyde Park Gate.

Julia, thirteen years younger than Leslie, was energetic, practical and altruistic – as she needed to be. In her recollections of 22 Hyde Park Gate, Virginia wrote that her mother believed that all men required 'an infinity of care'. Certainly Leslie required much care. And within six years Julia had borne four more children. So now there were eight children in the house, one of whom was, in Virginia's words, an idiot. This seemingly pejorative term was a recognized classification at the time for a person with the profound disabilities exhibited by Laura, born prematurely, slow to develop and unable to learn, facts that Leslie was slow to realize. Having fond memories of playing with her in Alpine meadows and of her early childish achievements that would, he felt sure in his paternal pride, lead to great things, he only recognized her problems after her kindergarten declared her uneducable. Unable to read, talkative to the point of unintelligibility and prone to unpredictability and inexplicable actions such as throwing scissors in the fire, her condition was such that it was deemed advisable to lodge her in a separate part of the house.

In all the records of this prolific family with its many cousins and branches, Laura Stephen is a conspicuous absence, and her story surprisingly scanty. After she was sixteen, she no longer lived at Hyde Park Gate, being placed in the care of a governess in her own home in Paignton, though joining the family at St Ives in the summers. At twenty-three, she was placed in the Earlswood Asylum for Idiots in Redhill, but four years later, in 1897, she was settled with Doctor Corner in Brook House, Southgate in north London. 'It seems to be good,' reported Leslie in his *Mausoleum Book*, 'but when I saw her the other day I was pained by her looks and ways. She is unable to recognize any of us clearly.' In fact, she had little opportunity for that, as it seems that her half-siblings never visited her. When she died in 1945, the home where she was then living knew of no relatives.

So from 1886 onwards, this was a household of seven children – still a large number to house. Two storeys had been added the year after their marriage on the basis of Julia's drawings – she wanted to save architect's fees, a detail that says much about the practicality of Virginia's mother. The brick-faced additions to the stucco-fronted house came in for condemnation later by the 1975 Survey of London: it was 'mutilated'.

A now-whitewashed house, divided into flats, it towers over its neighbours with its six storeys crowned by a Dutch-style gable. Inside it was dark. Julia made it darker through the use of much black paint and red velvet. Intricately patterned William Morris wallpapers added to the dimness. There was no electric light.

It was a house of 'innumerable small oddly shaped rooms', as Virginia remembered in her memoir 'Old Bloomsbury'. In the basement the servants' quarters – the kitchen and their sitting room – were separated from the wood-panelled dining room by a thick (red plush) curtain. The dining room, with its oak and red plush chairs, also served as the schoolroom.

Leading off the entrance hall with its fireplace was the drawing room, the engine-room of the house, divided by black folding doors, the colour emphasized by thin lines of scarlet. Busts and portraits were enhanced by crimson velvet. The 'thick sculptured folds of claret-coloured plush' curtains recur in *The Years*: the Pargiter family live in just such a house. The front half of the room, more open in aspect and more public, was used for entertaining: Sunday afternoon tea parties gathered round the oval table with its plate of spice buns. Eminent aged luminaries of Victorian academia and relatives mingled with young cousins and daughters of Julia's friends, like the three Lushington sisters (one of whom, Kitty, was the model for Clarissa Dalloway).

The back section was dimmed by Virginia creeper over the windows, 'a green cave', and was the more private room, where intimate encounters and emotional meetings took place. But amid this gloom and formality there is a glimpse of another intriguingly different atmosphere, a little side room that was largely the preserve of Vanessa and Virginia, close companions from the start (though Vanessa remembered how Virginia could quickly create an 'atmosphere of tense thundery gloom'). With

Virginia, aged two, with her mother Julia.

several windows and a skylight, this was 'a cheerful little room, almost entirely made of glass' as Vanessa described it, and it was here that the sisters perfected their different roles agreed from childhood, one that avoided the clash of competition – for alongside the sisterly affection there was also rivalry: Vanessa would be the artist, Virginia the author. There's a pleasing vignette, recorded in an early diary, in which Vanessa is standing drawing at an oak davenport while Virginia sits at a table beside her writing. In their cheerful side room, Vanessa remembered how she would paint, while Virginia read aloud. 'I can still hear much of George Eliot and Thackeray in her voice.'

Above the drawing rooms were bedrooms – significantly that of the parents, where all the Stephen children were born and where Julia and Leslie died: 'the sexual centre, the birth centre, the death centre of the house.' On the second floor were bedrooms and on the third, the nurseries. The night nursery was where all four Stephen children slept together, with a coal fire burning at night. Virginia used to fret if it were blazing, though Adrian liked seeing the flames flickering on the walls. Julia would settle this by folding a towel over the fireguard so that Virginia could not see the fire directly. A similar scene occurs in *To the Lighthouse*.

Between the nurseries and the attic bedrooms of the servants was Leslie's study, a fine large wood-panelled room with three long windows and lined with books. He worked in an armchair with a board across his knees, and the children in the nursery must have been conscious of him all the time above them, as he would drop books on the floor.

Lessons for the children were in the dining room. Their mother, Julia, taught them to read and write – not always a tranquil experience, Virginia recollected, as she had a quick temper. Leslie would coach them in mathematics (Vanessa said that Virginia counted on her fingers always) and Julia went on to teach the girls English and history, as well as a little French and Latin. The boys, to Virginia's enduring chagrin, were considered worthy of paid-for education. The girls did not even have a governess. Virginia's life was one long quest of self-education, which started with the growing frustration as her brothers were sent to school and she had to pick up what she could.

One can see from her letters that Virginia is desperately trying to keep up with Thoby, who, on holiday from his first school, told Virginia of the Greeks and their stories, as they walked together up and down the fine wooden and ironwork staircase. It must have been then that she determined to learn Greek.

When she was fifteen, she enrolled in Greek and Latin classes, which were offered in the King's College Department for Higher Education for Women in Kensington Square. Two years later she was having private lessons with Clara Pater, sister of essayist Walter Pater, in nearby Canning Place – her home described by Virginia as 'all blue china, Persian cats, and Morris wallpapers'.

Later, in 1900, she began to study in Hampstead with Janet Case, a Cambridge-trained classicist – and then lifelong friend, who, after she later moved to the New Forest, became a contributor to the *Manchester Guardian*'s Country Diary column. Janet Case's last contribution to Country Diary the month before she died in July 1937 refers to a visitor bearing armfuls of flowers and 'positively enveloped in green, like the "Jack-in-the-green" of our childhood days'; it is likely to have been Virginia who visited her often in her last illness and saw her in April that year.

The Round Pond in Kensington Gardens, where Virginia liked to sail her toy boat.

In contrast to the freedom of Cornwall, the excursions of the Stephen children were much more regulated. There were twice-daily trips to Kensington Gardens, through the Palace Gate entrance, with a nod to the gatekeeper in his green livery and gold-laced hat, perhaps purchasing a balloon for a penny from the old woman selling at that gate.

The usual walks – mostly dull, in Virginia's memory – would take her up Broad Walk to Round Pond or along Flower Walk: elements of those routes are recalled in *The Years*. It was inevitably unfavourably compared to St Ives. Once, the boat she used to sail on the Round Pond – a Cornish lugger, of course – suddenly sank. She did get it back the following spring: the pond was being dredged and the boat was brought up with duckweed in the dredging net. In excitement, she ran home full of the story of the happy reunion. What made this discovery even happier was that her mother made new sails for it, and her father rigged it: 'I remember seeing him fixing the sails to the yard-arm after dinner; and how interested he became and said, with his little snort, half laughing, something like "Absurd – what fun it is doing this!"'

This tender domestic scene contrasts with the grimness after her mother died. Julia Stephen, worn out by her self-abnegating life of good works as constant comforter and carer, succumbed to illness in the spring of 1895 and died of rheumatic fever on 5 May. It was a disaster for the family. The mourning widower was in constant grief and remorse, convinced that he had not told Julia he had loved her. His loud lamentations and groans were the soundtrack of that ever-gloomier house and he was insistent that his family appreciated his bereft status, and should share his feelings. Virginia said that 'a dark cloud settled over us', describing it as a period of Oriental gloom.

Leslie could no longer bear to return to St Ives – his stepson George went to St Ives to relinquish the lease – though there would still be family holidays. The first, wretched, trip of the motherless household was to Freshwater on the Isle of Wight, where their aunt lived. (It did, however, provide material for Virginia, who wrote a play, *Freshwater*, in 1923 to be resuscitated much later.)

The whole family was desolate, as the lynchpin of their life had been taken away – from Adrian, the youngest and the most cherished, to George, a man of twenty-seven and of the world, who felt impelled to now play a dominant role. Perhaps the two most overtly affected were Stella and Virginia, who was never, Vanessa thought, completely strong after an attack of whooping cough in her childhood.

Leslie, having relied utterly on Julia, turned to Stella, his stepdaughter, who capably and uncomplainingly stepped into her mother's shoes as organizer of the household, and comforter of the widower in addition to her self-appointed duties – she had helped set up a block of new buildings for the East End poor for which she was responsible. She took over supervision of Virginia's health too. The death of her mother had caused profound upset beyond grief – it was her first breakdown, and she was for a large part of her teenage years under the care of Dr Seton (who, coincidentally, was also the doctor for Leonard Woolf's family who, at that time, also lived in Kensington, at Lexham Gardens). He prescribed four hours of fresh air and exercise a day – and even gardening, so she bought a fork, spade, hoe and rake for 7/6d and began, without great enthusiasm, to till the small garden.

A VICTORIAN HOME – 22 HYDE PARK GATE

Stella Duckworth, Virginia's half-sister, who was thirteen years older.

Virginia went out with Stella on walks. In her diary of 1897, one of her first entries noted a trip to see a cousin, Jo Fisher, an architect of Stella's cottages, at his office. Even then Virginia was appraising the decor, as she would continue to do in the future, noting the advantageous position of the window overlooking the river and the 'hideous' green wallpaper, adorned with peacocks and lions.

Stella finally managed to detach herself from the grip of Leslie through the steady and persistent courtship of the likeable young solicitor Jack Hills, but the engagement was a long one as she negotiated her release from service. When they finally married in April 1897, she moved just two doors away to 24 Hyde Park Gate. However, she still kept up responsibility for Virginia, seeing her most days and holding inquisitions on her health, which were borne with irritation by Virginia – she was often 'tantrumical' – though one consolation was reading *Punch* magazine at Stella's house.

This state of affairs lasted barely any time at all: Stella had a mere three months of marriage before she died of peritonitis. It was yet another calamity for the family and for the health of Virginia, though there was no breakdown this time. Nine days after the burial of Stella in Highgate Cemetery (not attended by the Stephen children), the family adjourned to the pretty village of Painswick in Gloucestershire, renting the spacious vicarage (now a hotel) next to the churchyard which was famous for its ninety-nine yews. It was another mournful stay.

Thereafter the burden of the household fell on to Vanessa's shoulders, who – despite this responsibility – steadfastly followed her artistic bent, cycling off to art school after organizing the day's menus with Sophie – though, in truth, Vanessa had little say about these as Sophie did the ordering and shopping. Each Wednesday Vanessa had to present the books, as required by Leslie, and the accounts balanced. They rarely did, so there would be a weekly scene, where Lesley would rage about the expenditure and his impending penury, groaning and beating his breast the while. Vanessa, made of stern stuff, would stand unbending, unyielding, until Leslie wrote a cheque, while Virginia, appalled at her father's treatment of her sister, looked on, powerless. It was a scene that stayed with her all her life – she was still angry with her father at the age of fifty-nine.

# A VICTORIAN HOME – 22 HYDE PARK GATE

Virginia, with her father Leslie Stephen.

There was, nevertheless, a great bond between Leslie and Virginia. They appreciated each other intellectually and Leslie gave her free rein in his library. She was a voracious reader. 'Gracious, child, how you gobble,' he once remarked. When he suggested she read Macaulay's five-volume *History of England* for a stay in Brighton, she read two volumes in two weeks – and finished all a month later. They took occasional expeditions together, perhaps just to Kensington Gardens, where they 'lazily sat down in 2 armchairs' by the Serpentine watching the peacocks. Once, they visited Thomas Carlyle's house, after which she described his writing table with 'his pens, and scraps of manuscripts' and soundproof room (included in an essay 'Great Men's Houses' written in 1931 as part of a series about London for *Good Housekeeping*). There was even the surprisingly frivolous diversion of playing billiards with Leslie.

There were still the family holidays, including the duty trips to Brighton to visit Julia's sister, Mary Fisher. Warboys Rectory in Huntingdonshire on the edge of the Fens was a much more cheerful holiday in 1899. One excursion was to The Old Curiosity Shop in St Ives where she searched for a leather-bound volume for use as a diary, pasting her written pages into it. The one she chose was a tome by Isaac Watts: *Logick, or the Right Use of Reason in the Enquiry after Truth, with a Variety of Rules to guard against Error in the Affairs of Religion and Human Life as well as in the Sciences.* (There's no indication that she read it first.)

She wrote, too, of cycling through the Fens with Vanessa: 'This summer ranks among our happiest, I think.' The New Forest, where they stayed at Fritham, became a favourite. There was riding – there's a pleasing image of Virginia and Vanessa trotting about the forest looking for foxes. It is where Virginia first met Thoby's friend Lytton as the Stracheys lived nearby. And this is where Violet Dickinson came to stay in 1902. Virginia struck up a close friendship with her (presciently saying to her on that first occasion that she would like to be nursed by Violet if she were ill). She began a frequent correspondence with her, characterized by frankness and a rollicking humour. She was soon on intimate terms, calling it a 'romantic friendship' and addressing her as 'My Woman' and even sometimes 'My Child'. It satisfied Virginia's constant need for closeness. She took a close interest in the construction of the cottage that Violet was having built for herself at Burnham Wood, asking after the builders Chalky, Charlie and Quint, and enquiring about the wood where Violet had chosen the plot. She was also, crucially, sending Violet her literary exercises.

For most of her teenage years, Virginia spent much of her life on her own. Her half-brothers were at work, Thoby and Adrian away. After Vanessa had cycled off to art school, Virginia would go to the night nursery, now her bed-sitting room. The servants were in the basement, her father in his study above her. The former nursery, with its white walls and blue curtains, was the focal point of her personal life. She had Stella's old writing table, stained green and decorated with brown leaves, and a wicker chair. She also had what Vanessa described as 'a curious high desk at which she stood to write', possibly in imitation of Vanessa who had to stand to paint: Virginia did not want it to be thought that writing was any less arduous. She did occasionally follow other pursuits, such as bookbinding, an enthusiasm she shared with her cousin Emma

Vaughan, exchanging views on different materials for covers and on new techniques, such as trying out gold lettering on cloth. On occasion, she enjoyed home decoration: one letter she wrote to Violet explained that she was replying immediately though she had just been on the point of rolling up her sleeves to paint the floor.

But mostly she would spend the morning reading and studying. Her letters to Thoby, by then at Cambridge, were full of her efforts at self-education. He wrote to her of his new friends – Lytton Strachey, Leonard Woolf, Clive Bell, John Maynard Keynes (always called Maynard), E. M. Forster, known as Morgan – and she was deeply envious of his cerebral pursuits, his intellectual friendships and conversations.

But this was a firmly Victorian household, 'a complete model of Victorian society,' as she wrote in 'A Sketch of the Past'. Even her half-brothers, teenagers when Julia married Leslie, followed Victorian conventions and rules. Virginia could only escape the pressures of society in the mornings. Vanessa and Virginia were expected for tea in the afternoon. If there were guests, they would have to entertain them and mediate, as Leslie was very deaf now and used an ear trumpet. In the evening they would be required to dress for dinner. After that, George, self-appointed head of the household, insisted on introducing the two girls into society, first Vanessa and, when she finally rebelled, then Virginia. Many excruciating evenings had to be endured. But they were made worse by George's behaviour when home. Over-affectionate, to say the least, he would creep into Virginia's bedroom late at night and fling himself on the bed hugging and fondling her. Whatever his intentions, it left its mark on her.

The house in the last years of Leslie's life was dominated by illness after he was diagnosed in 1902 with cancer, the year he was offered a knighthood. Even as his health declined, there were still holidays: a house at Netherhampton in Salisbury, where she had a vast whitewashed attic to herself, met with Virginia's approval, but she had a scathing view of the last family holiday in Surrey, thinking it a charlatan county: 'everyone artistic seems to retire here, and build a red-brick house with sham Elizabethan white and black.'

Towards the end, the family sat with their father day after day, alongside a phalanx of grieving relatives. But at the same time the Stephen children were compelled to make plans for the future. The death of Sir Leslie Stephen in February 1904 marked the end of a Victorian way of life.

# 'The Light and the Air' – Bloomsbury

*'Home at last to our native Bloomsbury'*

---

No time was lost in shaking off the shackles after the death of Leslie. Just five days later, the Stephen children – Vanessa, Thoby, Virginia and Adrian – along with George Duckworth travelled to Manorbier in Wales, where they stayed for almost a month. The seaside village in Pembrokeshire is now favoured as a 'surf spot' but then was truly isolated with a handful of houses and a medieval castle, complete with battlements and towers, on a cliff over the sea. The 'splendid wild country' reminded Virginia of the Cornish coast around St Ives, and the siblings spent much of their time walking, but also reading, drawing and writing. It was in Manorbier, as Virginia recollected years later, that she had the first inkling of the first book she would write, as she walked along the edge of the sea.

They were back in London only briefly before travelling to Venice in April, this time with Gerald, and thence to Florence, where they met up with Violet Dickinson – and many others from their social circle, cousins and aunt included. The return journey broke at Paris where there were meetings in cafés with Thoby's friends, including Clive Bell – and a visit to Rodin's studio. By this stage, Virginia's mood was deteriorating – she found Paris less congenial than Vanessa. However, the sequence of journeys provided respite from the constant gloom and stress of the last months of Leslie's illness. For all the Stephens it represented a clear marker for the beginning of a new life. And a new home.

46 Gordon Square, in Bloomsbury, was in 1904 the first independent home for the Stephen siblings. The plaque is for John Maynard Keynes, who lived here from 1916 to 1946.

This had already been discussed. Vanessa and Virginia felt they should leave 22 Hyde Park Gate and, to their relief, they found that Gerald thought so too: his view was that he and George were a generation older and that the Stephens should make their lives independently. He even suggested Bloomsbury as a place to consider. They had visited Bloomsbury before Leslie's death but Virginia had been unimpressed, finding it cold and gloomy (it had been December). In January, they had viewed another house, one that had pleased Virginia but was too small. Jack, their brother-in-law, who went with them, said that they would never get anyone to dine with them in such a neighbourhood. Peopled by students, journalists, artists and authors, there was a much more liberal atmosphere – something that did not meet with the approval of strait-laced relatives. There was also a looming anxiety about George. Gerald had happily cast off from the family to live independently, but George, still in his self-appointed role as paterfamilias, was vacillating about his duty to superintend the new household. However, by fortunate and timely circumstance, he met Lady Margaret Herbert, proposed, and was married to her that summer in Somerset.

Vanessa, full of determination and enterprise even at twenty-four, headed the search for a new London home and discovered it in Gordon Square, far removed from the formality of Kensington, and a great deal cheaper. The five-storey terraced house was also a great contrast to their former home, full of light and overlooking a square full of plane trees.

Having their own home liberated the Stephens in a way that would have been inconceivable if they had remained in Kensington, where they would have been in thrall to their relatives and a still-Victorian society. Reordering their domestic environment and having control of their own affairs, with the ability to see their own friends and to work as they pleased, gave them a passport to a completely different life.

By the autumn, the house in Hyde Park Gate had been left behind. It was mortgaged and then rented out – apart from their own expenses, there were those incurred by the asylum for Laura. Much of its furniture was sold to Harrods and by October 46 Gordon Square had become the new home of the Stephen family.

But the move was made without Virginia. The day after their return from Paris, on 10 May, she had had a breakdown. The loss of her father, to whom she had been close despite his domineering and stifling emotional behaviour, had tilted the fragile balance of her mind. After the death of her mother it was her half-sister Stella who had nursed her through her collapse. After the death of her father it was Stella's friend Violet who took on the same maternal role. Now under the supervision of Dr Savage and in the care of three nurses, Virginia was taken to Burnham Wood. There she moved into a confused and terrifying mental world. She refused to eat, could hear birds singing in Greek, and had visions of a malevolent King Edward VII lurking in the garden. She descended to such a desperate state that she threw herself out of a window, though it was not high enough to cause her harm. Septimus Warren Smith, the poet in *Mrs Dalloway*, who is deranged by his experiences in the First World War, exhibits the same symptoms.

Burnham Wood, the home of Violet Dickinson who cared for Virginia here during her breakdown after her father's death.

After three months, when she had largely recovered, she was eager to return to her normal life in London, where she could 'read herself into peace', and longing to begin writing again. But Dr Savage decreed otherwise, feeling London would at that stage be too exciting. So after a short holiday with her siblings, who were staying at Teversal Manor in Nottinghamshire, a seventeenth-century manor house (widely considered to have been reproduced by D. H. Lawrence as Wragby Hall in *Lady Chatterley's Lover*), she went with great reluctance to stay in Cambridge with her aunt Caroline Emilia, Leslie's devoted sister, at her small house, The Porch. There she had the consolation of helping the historian Frederic Maitland with research for his biography of Leslie Stephen, but the prescribed peace and quiet with her aunt, variously dubbed 'The Quaker' or 'The Nun', soon became too much for her. She found the incessant mourning over Leslie very trying, and she engaged in long-distance disputes with Vanessa about returning to London, and Vanessa's adherence to Dr Savage's view that Virginia needed more rest.

Violet Dickinson, nearly six feet tall, took a maternal interest in Virginia.

Allowed back for a few days in November, as she had to go to the dentist, she was at the farewell dinner on 17 November that Thoby gave for Leonard Woolf, before he set sail for Ceylon where he was to be an administrator in the Ceylon Civil Service. (Leonard remembers Virginia on that occasion as being perfectly silent and looking quite ill.) He had met her once before at Trinity in

Cambridge, along with Vanessa, both in white dresses and big hats, when they visited Thoby in 1903: 'their beauty literally took one's breath away.' Virginia made another significant contact in this period – with *The Guardian*, a weekly journal for members of the clergy and like-minded readers. Virginia had been sending her 'literary exercises' to Violet for a while, and Kathleen Lyttelton, the women's editor of *The Guardian,* was a friend of Violet's. Virginia began to write reviews to send her.

After that brief taste of her new home, she went to Giggleswick in Yorkshire to stay with her cousin Will Vaughan and his wife Madge (who had stayed with the Stephen family for some months in 1889, when she was twenty and Virginia, aged seven, had a crush on her). While in Yorkshire she visited the Brontë Parsonage and wrote the essay 'Haworth, November 1904', which was eventually to mark her entry into the world of journalism. So her career was beginning, but her frustration was great as, in London, Vanessa was in the throes of busily settling into the new life, organizing the new home and describing it as 'a company of the young, all free, all beginning life in new surroundings'.

Vanessa had started with vigour to create a different environment, eschewing wallpapers and the William Morris look in favour of distempering the walls in white, brightening with the brilliant, vivid splashes of strategically placed scarves or shawls. Instead of the red plush of Hyde Park Gate, there were green and white chintzes everywhere. (Virginia thought them delightful.) She began to give full rein to her sense of colour: in a London square where dignity was demonstrated by the front doors of grey, dark blue or black, the door of 46 was vermilion.

Vanessa found it 'exhilarating to have left the house in which there had been so much gloom and depression, to have come to these white walls, large windows opening on to trees and lawns, to have one's own rooms, to be master of one's own time.' She kept Virginia in touch with her changes, feeling rather pleased with her arrangements of the pictures brought from the house. In the hall was 'a row of celebrities': on one side William Herschel, Charles Darwin, Lord Alfred Tennyson, Robert Browning, their father, and, on the other, a set of Julia Margaret Cameron's portraits of their mother. She mentioned that she had bought a red carpet for the sitting room and told Virginia about the rooms that she would have.

She bought her sister a new worktable – 'very solid and steady, and nice to look at'.

It was not until the New Year that Virginia was given a clean bill of health by Dr Savage and finally included in the Gordon Square household. To Virginia, Bloomsbury was then, a year after her disparaging remarks, 'the most beautiful, the most exciting, the most romantic place in the world.' She found it much more interesting than Kensington: there was always an art gallery to visit, a concert to attend. She wrote how she found herself lunching and dining, 'loitering about bookshops' and coming home to Gordon Square to find visitors, all of a rather more congenial nature than at Hyde Park Gate. She loved to go on long walks, often with Vanessa's sheepdog, Gurth, to Regent's Park (ever afterwards a favourite spot), or to Oxford Street, returning 'home at last to our native Bloomsbury'. It was the beginning of her walking habit, so important to her and her writing throughout her life.

This early Victorian house in a Bohemian part of London represented freedom and informality: the choice to serve coffee instead of tea, to avoid napkins. The significance of these small gestures cannot be underestimated. But the house itself was key. 'The light and the air after the rich red gloom of Hyde Park Gate was a revelation,' Virginia wrote. Not least, perhaps, because in this house there was electric light, a matter of marvel. Even the roar of traffic that permeated Gordon Square was an attraction after the muffled silence of Hyde Park Gate. Virginia did revisit her childhood home, which she'd left as a fully functioning and furnished house in the spring and was now empty of all its associations: it was probably a relief to find that it did not affect her, though she knew the marks on the walls where the bookcase had stood, where the writing-table had stood, and thought of herself sitting there. It was scene recreated later in *The Years*, when Eleanor Pargiter left Abercorn Terrace ('The white light of the snow. . . showed up the marks on the wall, where the furniture had stood, where the pictures had hung.') But – like Eleanor – she did not regret the move.

Virginia happily settled in to her top-floor bedroom and sitting room with a view across the plane trees in Gordon Square. Her first priority was sorting out the heating: all the rooms had coal fires, and she had to make a trip to Lincoln's Inn Fields to get a grate made; early purchases were a brass coal scuttle and fire

Virginia's cherished view from her rooms on the top floor were of the trees in Gordon Square.

irons 'to match my fender, which is a source of real joy to me'. She went on other shopping expeditions – coveting a 'great hooded chair' and rejecting it on grounds of cost 'and moreover shuts out the light', but acquiring a looking glass to set over her desk, which would, she thought, liven up the room. She hung her pictures, turned the bed round. On a more daily, domestic note, she enjoyed visits to Covent Garden market for vegetables. For a short while, she had a cat – possibly the Blue Persian kitten that she had 'interviewed' the previous November while staying with her aunt in Cambridge.

Violet sent her a fine table that could be adjusted to different heights – it lent 'such an air' to the room and would, Virginia was certain, 'serve for all the books I shall ever write'. She bought a bookcase, and, once settled in, began to read and write more intensively again. Nurse Traill, who had cared for her during her

Thoby, Virginia's older brother, began the evening gatherings of the friends he had made at Cambridge: this was the beginning of what became known as the Bloomsbury Group.

recent breakdown, was still in occasional attendance, often just for a fifteen-minute check-up and chat.

There was also a new social life. On 1 March she and her siblings were hard at work preparing for their housewarming party. Virginia was pleased with the result: 'the rooms as empty as a moonlit sky; & brilliant with light & sweet flowers' and satisfied with the party that, despite moments of difficulty, was on the whole 'garrulous & successful I think'. As it didn't finish until after midnight, she was probably right.

The first of the Thursday Evenings began that month. Thoby wanted to continue his Cambridge discussions, and so invited his friends for conversation over cocoa and biscuits. The first, on 16 March, consisted of only Saxon Sydney-Turner, a reputedly clever though very silent graduate, but the following week nine people came and stayed until 1a.m. Among this group were Lytton Strachey, who became a close friend, and Clive Bell, who proposed marriage to Vanessa that summer but was turned down. Though the evenings were characterized then by long, perhaps thoughtful, silences rather than brilliant, scintillating debate, it indicated the beginnings of what came to be known as the Bloomsbury Group.

Virginia was also working hard. In December her review of *The Son of Royal Langbrith*, a novel by the prolific but now little-known American writer W. D. Howells, had appeared in *The Guardian*, followed the next week by her first published article, 'Haworth November 1904'. The cheque for both was £2 7s 6d – she had proudly become a freelance journalist and – when getting a library ticket for the Dr Williams' Library in Gordon Square (it is still there, as part of University College London) – described herself as a journalist who wanted to read history. She was writing fiction too – a short story 'Phyllis and Rosamond', published in 1906, about two sets of girls, one from Kensington visiting the other in Bloomsbury, encapsulated the contrasts in her own life.

Virginia was now writing reviews regularly, delivering thirty articles in 1905. For two years this liberated and productive time was ideal. She took a post at Morley College for Working Men and Women at the urging of its Vice-Principal and social reformer Mary Sheepshanks. It must have been the first time that she engaged with working people who were not servants. Her brief was to give talks about books and pictures, which developed into composition, literature and history. It was a task she diligently continued for two years and, though she did not find it very rewarding, it provided useful structure in a freelance life.

One thing a successful freelance life does require is a congenial home – certainly provided by 46 Gordon Square. Virginia took particular pleasure in her quarters: she wrote to Madge Vaughan of the fire and electric light, as well as her beloved leather-bound books 'standing up so handsome in their shelves'. Most importantly, was the 'huge mass of manuscripts and letters and proof-sheets and pens and inks over the floor and everywhere'. For Virginia this was the perfect combination. 'Tomorrow week they will be bad enough for a general clearance; then I start to tidy and gradually work myself up into a happy frenzy of litter.'

There were excursions, mainly dictated by term times for this period. She went to Portugal and Spain with Adrian in the Easter vacation: the journey there took a week by boat – an experience that fuelled Virginia's first novel, *The Voyage Out*. In August, the four Stephens went back to Cornwall, where they stayed until October. On their first evening they made a twilight pilgrimage to their beloved Talland House. They revisited old haunts and enjoyed being remembered by some of the townsfolk. They even, for the first time ever in all their years of visits to St Ives, heard the Huer's cry and saw the shoals of pilchards come.

In August 1906, in another reminder of family holidays, Vanessa and Virginia rented Blo' Norton Hall in East Harling, Norfolk, a moated Elizabethan manor house 'striped with oak bars inside, old staircases, ancestral vats and portraits'. (It is still available for rent, though at a rather more luxurious rate.) It provided the setting for Virginia's (long) short story 'The Journal of Mistress Joan Martyn', written while she was there.

But this halcyon period came to a tragic turning point: in the early autumn of 1906 the family, accompanied by Violet, went on a long-anticipated expedition to Greece, but it was disrupted by misfortune when Vanessa fell ill, at one point confined to bed in Athens for two weeks. Plans were resumed, disrupted, rearranged, and then, Thoby having returned to England earlier as planned, the rest of the party made their way to Constantinople where Vanessa relapsed (and Virginia had time for a little shopping for flame-coloured material to drape chairs). They eventually came back to London on the Orient Express. But as Vanessa was put to bed (she was eventually diagnosed with appendicitis), the news was bad – Thoby was now ill. His illness, initially misdiagnosed as malaria, was typhoid: he died on 20 November. Two days after his death, Vanessa accepted another proposal of marriage from Clive Bell so, in the space of two days, Virginia had lost two pillars of her existence – her cherished elder brother; and, through marriage, also her sister, the single most important person in her life. She would be deprived of the protective bulwark of Gordon Square, as it was to become the marital home of the Bells. Catastrophe had once again intervened. Life and home were changing unpredictably.

And yet, showing a resilience that would not have been thought possible, Virginia, now twenty-five, set about house-hunting for herself and Adrian, two years younger. Perhaps it was the very nature of the settled and liberated tenancy of Gordon Square, an environment so unlike the trapped confinement of Hyde Park Gate, that had freed her to explore other homes, other places – a pursuit that she was to enjoy for years to come. It was Vanessa who had found Gordon Square, but now Virginia – who had hitherto relied so much on her older sister – took control. She wanted a house that was at least ten minutes away: to live closer would, she thought, be a mistake. She spent January searching and found a pleasant-looking 1830s house on the west side of Fitzroy Square, with arched windows and a balcony. It had electric light, the landlord would put in a bath and promised to paint the exterior. It was within easy reach of Gordon Square, which remained a focus for friends and family: years later Lytton wrote to Virginia that 'very soon I foresee that the whole Square will become a sort of College'. And so it did: it is now at the heart of Birkbeck College and University College London (UCL).

29 Fitzroy Square had been the home of the playwright George Bernard Shaw's mother until that year and was where, from 1887 until his marriage in 1898, Shaw had lived in what he called 'this most repulsive house' (though this might have been due to his own habits – his future wife, Charlotte, had been shocked to see the room in which Shaw worked 'in a perpetual state of dirt and disorder'). Though this was the only London square to have the distinction of being designed by Robert Adam, the location seemed even less desirable than

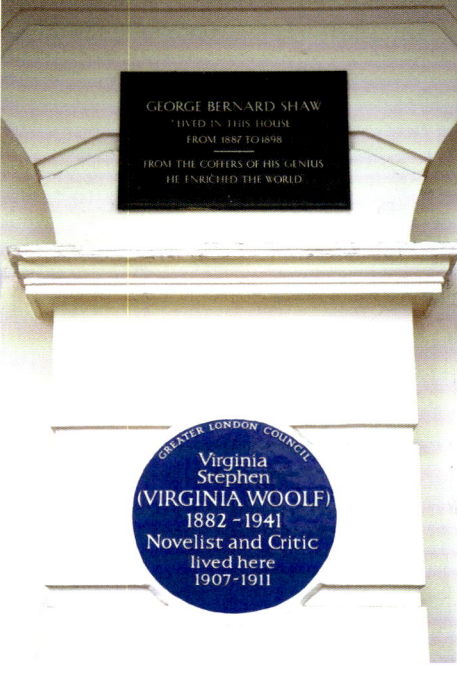

The playwright and critic George Bernard Shaw, who had lived at 29 Fitzroy Square from 1887 to 1898.

The plaques commemorate Virginia and George Bernard Shaw.

Gordon Square to Virginia's refined relations and friends. Even Violet disapproved of the neighbourhood, though Virginia argued her corner, pointing out the school, hospitals and other respectable institutions around. Sturdy though her response was, the reaction infected her with enough alarm to consult the police about the neighbourhood. However, she made an offer, and after tramping round the house with a builder, who found all satisfactory, felt vindicated 'as I am supposed to have a nose for a house'. In March 1907, Virginia moved in with Adrian and embarked on running a household.

Of course, she did not have to actually manage the house by herself: Sophie Farrell, the family cook who had moved from Hyde Park Gate to Gordon Square, chose to follow Virginia rather than stay with Vanessa. Virginia, she said, was

Sophie Farrell, the family cook at 22 Hyde Park Gate, who followed the Stephen children to Gordon Square and then moved with Virginia to Fitzroy Square as her need was greater than Vanessa's.

'such a harum scarum thing, she wouldn't know if they sold her. She don't know what she has on her plate.' Virginia had actually taken Sophie with her when house-hunting, and, as Virginia told Violet, she had approved of the Fitzroy Square house 'in every particular'. Maud the housemaid came too. So when Virginia wrote 'I think housekeeping is what I do best' and 'I mean to run our house on very remarkable lines', these have to be taken in the context of a good support team.

It is true, however, that she was mistress of the house, and could choose the decoration herself: she sat on a cupboard in the drawing room directing the painters, found great satisfaction in choosing the curtains (red brocade), carpets (bright green) and in buying old furniture. At first, curiously, she wanted to keep

the main room free of armchairs, but this plan was superseded by the desire for comfort. There was some regret about the noise of traffic, but double windows were installed. Virginia had a whole floor to herself: her sitting room had 'great pyramids of books, with trailing mists between them; partly dust, and partly cigarette-smoke.' The drawing room was later decked out in purple. She made a tie for Adrian out of purple silk.

This new arrangement was not the same as sharing a home with Vanessa. Adrian, as the youngest of the family was only eleven when his mother died and Virginia did want to make a 'cheerful' home for him. She felt a responsibility for him, especially now that he had lost his brother, and had spent the first Christmas without Thoby and Vanessa alone with him in the New Forest in quite a convivial way. She had once said to Violet that he was one of the people that made it worthwhile to live and be happy. But he was not a soul mate. And Virginia became increasingly aware that he looked up to Vanessa in a way that he did not to her, which rankled. Later in life Virginia had some regrets that she had mostly sided with her adored older sister and brother, rather than forming a pair with Adrian, but they were temperamentally very unalike. She described him once as being '15 years younger than all the rest of us'.

Social occasions with the Gordon Square household included the inauguration of the Play Reading Society with John Vanbrugh's *The Relapse* and continued on Friday evenings with Shakespeare and Ibsen. These ameliorated the difficulties of sharing with Adrian, where debates tended to degenerate into horseplay. What might start out as reasoned discussion often ended in juvenile insults and, on occasion, an exchange of fusillades of butter pats.

Vanessa and Virginia contrived to continue their close connection, seeing each other several times a week, though there was a significant change in their relationship when Vanessa's first baby, Julian, was born. In April 1908 Virginia was staying in lodgings in St Ives, where the Bells joined her. The holiday for Virginia had not started well: the landlady had nine children, and their sitting room was

29 Fitzroy Square became the venue for the revived Thursday Evenings, with Thoby's friends from Cambridge as well as Virginia's own contacts.

Fitzroy Square, with its circular garden within, was the only London square designed by Robert Adam.

next to the room where Virginia was trying to write. There were letters from Vanessa detailing all the paraphernalia, including cradle and bath, needed for such a visit that would require 'a short vehicle to bring me and nurse and baby from the station with 1 box and perambulator' and another for the rest. And then there was the presence of the infant himself. Afterwards, Virginia said she doubted that she would ever have a baby: 'the amount of business that has to be got through before you can enjoy it is dismaying.' But what was truly dismaying was that she had been displaced from prime place in Vanessa's affections.

    Clive and Virginia found common cause in resentment at Vanessa's total absorption in the baby. They took long walks together, discussing Virginia's concerns over her writing. He was a helpful literary confidant but the conversations developed into a flirtation that continued beyond the holiday. Clive, a lifelong

Lothario, made great play for Virginia, who couldn't resist the flattery and responded playfully. With great self-control, Vanessa, who must have been deeply hurt, tolerated the relationship, treating it with levity. The flirtation remained just that. But for Vanessa, the key element of trust was lost. Though the sisters continued to be close, that remained a shadow. (In *Deceived with Kindness*, Angelica, Vanessa's daughter, wrote of how she sensed a wariness in Vanessa 'and on Virginia's side a desperate plea for forgiveness'.) Virginia maintained her always intense correspondence with Vanessa – even when staying in Wells that summer, while chivvying Vanessa for a letter, she fantasized that Vanessa would have a country house with a cottage at the bottom of the garden for her: 'There I shall have a room, a great table, some books and a looking glass, beside a curious cabinet, full of small drawers, in which your children shall search for secrets.'

Undoubtedly the years after Vanessa's marriage were difficult for Virginia, dependent as she was on her older sister, and there must have been a good deal of loneliness in sharing a house with her unappreciative young brother, though she steadfastly practised self-sufficiency. On Christmas Eve 1909 she had a yearning for Cornwall and at 12.30 realized that there was a train at 1p.m. from Paddington. Extraordinarily, she made it, even if missing a few essentials (spectacles, chequebook, coat) and spent the next few days at the Lelant Hotel

Badger Inn in Lelant, near St Ives, was formerly the Lelant Hotel, where Virginia spent Christmas 1909 on her own.

Lady Ottoline Morrell, society hostess, who came to one of Virginia and Adrian's Evenings and reciprocated by inviting everyone there to a soirée at her home in Bedford Square.

(now the Badger Inn) in Lelant, a village close to St Ives. She listened to carols, walked on the beach, climbed Trencrom, 'coming back past lighted windows to one's tea and book'. She thrilled to the solitude and congratulated herself on her decision.

Back in London, she and Adrian tried to be companionable, having revived the Thursday Evenings with an expanded membership. There were the Cambridge young men, but Virginia included her own contacts, such as her old Greek tutor,

Janet Case, and Mary Sheepshanks. A conversation at one of these evenings led to Virginia volunteering to stuff envelopes for the Women's Suffrage Movement, where she met Margaret Llewelyn Davies, who was to play an important part in her and Leonard's life. Another long relationship began when the society hostess Lady Ottoline Morrell turned up at one of the evenings, and soon afterwards invited all the attendees to her own 'At Home' in Bedford Square, full of luminaries like Winston Churchill, Augustus John and Bertrand Russell. Thereafter, Virginia was a frequent guest at the house parties Ottoline held at her Oxfordshire home, the Jacobean Garsington Manor, with its famed sitting room (its deep red walls were commended by Virginia) and its glorious gardens.

One new recruit to Virginia's circle was the artist Duncan Grant, who moved into 21 Fitzroy Square, renting two rooms to use as his studio – though it was actually Maynard Keynes, one of the Bloomsbury Group and now making his name as an economist, paying the rent, as they were having an affair. Duncan began to use Virginia and Adrian's house as a home from home. He would turn up on Thursdays for cocoa, buns and whisky. It was not long before he had transferred his affections to Adrian – a defection that Maynard seemed to take in good part.

It was from this home that the notorious Dreadnought Hoax was launched. It was Adrian's idea, along with his friend Horace Cole, the instigator of many practical jokes. The plan was to dress up as a delegation from the court of Abyssinia and to fool the Royal Navy, by inveigling themselves on to HMS *Dreadnought*, the flagship of the Home Fleet. Virginia, asked to take part two days beforehand, was delighted. Dressing as 'Prince Mendax' in turban, embroidered caftan and with blackened face and beard, she joined Adrian (the interpreter), Horace (the Foreign Office official) and Duncan (another Abyssinian) as they set out from Paddington station. It was an immense success in that the telegram announcing this sudden visit of the Emperor of Abyssinia and his entourage was (rather incredibly) accepted and their disguises were not penetrated. They were shown round the boat, declined refreshments (afraid that their beards might detach) and returned to London. The matter might have ended there, the jape had worked and that was satisfaction enough, but Horace Cole could not bear to keep it quiet and went to the newspapers. There was, inevitably, reproval from the

The Dreadnought Hoax was front-page news in 1910. Virginia, dressed as 'Prince Mendax', is on the far left.

Stephen relatives, and the Navy did not take it well. But all died down. In July 1940, Virginia regaled Rodmell Women's Institute with an account of it, causing much mirth.

Throughout the high jinks and the social gatherings, Virginia continued with her journalism: she still wrote for *The Guardian* and contributed to *The Cornhill Magazine* for a while, until a piece she was particularly pleased with was turned down. However, her main source of work became the *Times Literary Supplement*, whose editor Bruce Richmond plied her with books to review, a relationship that was to last thirty years. On the whole this worked satisfactorily – though she was infuriated when he demanded she change a word that he deemed unseemly in a review of Henry James's ghost stories. (The word was 'lewd' and she eventually replaced it with 'obscene'.) Still, that was not as bad as the occasion – familiar to freelance journalists – when she found her copy mutilated: she had supplied an article entitled 'A Plague of Essays' to the journal *Academy and Literature*, to find that, when published, the title and text had been changed and it had been cut in half.

But more important to her was the start of a novel, first called *Melymbrosia* and later *The Voyage Out*. She had begun it in 1907, and continued it the following year during a stay in Manorbier, the place where she had had the first glimmer of inspiration. She took a room at Sea View, but her landlady negotiated day-access to a house a minute or so away, which had a room with a desk, where she wrote 100 pages. She asked the advice of Clive, which, of course, he was delighted to give. It was to go through many drafts before she was to submit it for publication.

Alongside this busy working and social life, there was considerable pressure on Virginia to marry. She chafed at this, but she herself expected it, keeping Vanessa, still, despite all, her closest companion, informed on possible liaisons. Her strongest passions had been for women: Vanessa, Madge Vaughan, Violet. And certainly her experience with her half-brother George had made her wary. However, what was most important to Virginia was intellectual equality. There was one person whom she could and did consider living with – Lytton, and in a moment of aberration (his relationships were mostly with men) he did propose to her in 1909, regretting it almost immediately, which Virginia sensed, and they

Virginia with Lytton Strachey, one of her greatest friends, at Garsington Manor, the Oxfordshire home of Lady Ottoline Morrell.

detached themselves from each other the next day. It was then that Lytton, who had maintained a frequent correspondence with Leonard Woolf in Ceylon, slyly suggested that Leonard should marry Virginia. Virginia had other suitors, there was even a proposal or two, but she was not in the end enticed by any of them. For Leonard, the seed had been sown.

Meanwhile, Virginia, deep in the composition of *The Voyage Out* and close to its completion (a time that was always to be perilous to her state of mind), fell ill again. Vanessa and Clive did what they could and booked the Moat House at Blean near Canterbury. But the holiday did not calm her jangled nerves, and after their return to London Vanessa consulted Dr Savage, who decreed a month of complete rest at Burley House in Twickenham, at 15 Cambridge Park, a nursing home for women with 'nervous disorders' run by Miss Jean Thomas. A substantial house built of Suffolk brick, with a flight of steps to the front door, it did not appeal to Virginia. 'The ugliness of the house is almost inexplicable. . . white and mottled green and red,' she wrote to Vanessa, but the large walled grounds and closeness to Marble Hill Park made some compensation. She still worked on her novel: the illness with its hallucinations and fever experienced by Rachel in *The Voyage Out* probably drew on her time there.

That August Virginia returned to Cornwall on a walking tour accompanied by Jean Thomas, before joining Vanessa and family (Julian's brother had been born) at Studland in Dorset. She wrote proudly to Violet that she made her own breakfast and had eggs and milk delivered. She said, with a sense of revelation, that milk went sour very quickly. 'Butter and bacon however will with luck keep a week.' It was October before she returned to Fitzroy Square. She had regained her health, but the appeal of the calm of the countryside was obvious to her – and especially to her friends and doctor. When she and Adrian spent Christmas that year in Lewes, she began to look for a place to rent in Sussex, and found a semi-detached house in Firle on the South Downs. Before long, she was inviting friends, old and new: Leonard Woolf, for example. He had returned from Ceylon on leave in June and after she met him three weeks later at the Bells' home, she asked him too. When he joined her at Firle that September, they went for long walks, and talked, Leonard said, until the early hours. That weekend they came across another house for rent, Asheham (sometimes spelled Asham, especially by the Woolfs), an isolated Regency house that captivated her. She and Vanessa signed the lease in October.

October was the month, too, that she was due to leave Fitzroy Square. Virginia and Adrian had decided to try a different mode of living – with friends. The 'Bedford Square plan' for a house for communal living was under discussion, but they were to move to a house in Brunswick Square, owned by the Foundling Hospital (now replaced by the Foundling Museum, next to Coram's Fields) that had a portfolio of property in Bloomsbury: in 1790, fields belonging to the hospital had been released for house building – Brunswick Square was built first, followed by Mecklenburgh Square, its twin to the east. Brunswick Square is much altered

Virginia at Garsington Manor, a house she greatly admired, describing it as 'a floating palace'. She was a frequent guest at the house parties there.

now, with a shopping centre to the west, and the north terrace (which included 38) demolished and replaced by the UCL School of Pharmacy. But then it was a welcome change from Fitzroy Square – quieter and with a pleasant graveyard (now St George's Gardens).

The plan was for Adrian and Virginia to live there with friends. Maynard (now a fellow of King's College, Cambridge) would maintain a London base on the ground floor, which would also provide a studio for Duncan. The first floor would be for Adrian, still in a relationship with Duncan, who covered Adrian's sitting room with pictures of life-sized tennis players in the style of Matisse's dancers. Virginia would be above, and the top floor was to be offered to Leonard Woolf.

Of course the plan caused ructions. Living as young people in a family without chaperones had been frowned upon. Living in Gordon Square had been bad enough, and Fitzroy Square was worse. But to live, as Virginia was intending now, with four young men, only one of whom was related, was beyond the pale. Half-brother, aunts and family friends, like Violet, were scandalized.

However, Virginia and Adrian were not to be dissuaded, and with impeccable organization allocated the rooms and made up the ground rules. Virginia took control, in charge of the rents and the contributions to housekeeping, wages and meals. She drew up the 'Scheme of the House', which was a novel one – and, of course, depended on the services of Sophie and Maud, who had come to their new home. The Kitchen Instruction Tablet would be placed in the hall each day for 'inmates' to append their initials against each meal required. Meals on trays would be served in the hall at 9a.m., 1p.m., 4.30p.m. and 8p.m. Each person was to take their tray to their rooms and return it *'as soon as the meal is finished'*.

Her friendship with Leonard developed swiftly. They each worked in the morning – Leonard was writing a novel too, *The Village in the Jungle,* based on his experiences in Ceylon – and after lunch together they would walk and talk in the afternoon. They shared many of the same views, but also ideals and dedication to hard work. Neither of them was over-interested in money nor in elaborate lifestyles and they had little respect for convention. For Virginia, acutely intellectual herself, his intellect and his confidence – without arrogance – remained always deeply attractive. He was extraordinarily independent-minded, always attentive to his family but unmoved by the mores that might have been expected to apply.

It wasn't long before Leonard was completely committed; Virginia, ever cautious, was less so. He spent Christmas Day at Gordon Square with the Bells and Virginia, and then left London to visit a friend in Somerset. On 10 January he sent a telegram to Virginia saying he must see her for an hour the next afternoon at 38 Brunswick Square. He proposed marriage, and then returned to Somerset. Virginia was uncertain – they engaged in intense and sometimes anguished correspondence, discussing their feelings. For his part he told her that it was not just her beauty that he loved, he said – important though that was – it was her mind and character. 'We like one another, we like the same kinds of things & people, we are both intelligent & above all it is realities which we understand & which are important for us.'

Her replies indicate that she was tempted – but conflicted. Virginia set out the pros and cons: desire for companionship and children; anger at the strength of his desire; her instability; his Jewishness that made him seem so foreign. Unsurprisingly, the ferment left her ill again; she retreated to Twickenham for two weeks, and spent much of the spring recuperating at Asheham. As for Leonard, he applied for an extension to his leave, was initially refused, and then resigned. It was a momentous decision, for his stock was high, and he was turning his back on what was likely to have been an illustrious career. But he was now determined to try to marry Virginia if he could. A risky endeavour, but one he was in no doubt about.

In May 1912, finally overcoming her extremes of indecision, Virginia agreed to marry him.

Virginia and Leonard at Dalingridge Place, home of her half-brother George Duckworth, after their decision to marry.

# Marriage and Partnership – Hogarth House

## *'This beautiful and loveable house'*

Virginia and Leonard were married on 10 August 1912 at St Pancras Registry Office, near St Pancras Old Church in Camden. It was planned, as she explained in a letter to Lady Ottoline Morell, 'quite suddenly', since Vanessa and Clive were leaving London. (Clive wasn't at the ceremony, but hosted a lunch afterwards in Gordon Square.) Other guests were her half-brother George, her aunt Mary Fisher, and friends Duncan Grant, Saxon Sydney-Turner, Roger Fry and Fred Etchells. It was a strange collection, omitting closer friends and all of Leonard's family. (His mother bitterly resented her exclusion.)

Virginia relished the simplicity of the occasion – 'You stand up and repeat two sentences, and then sign your name' – and the fact that it thundered throughout the short ceremony. Leonard was struck by the fact that the window overlooked a cemetery, which made him think of the words unuttered in this civil ceremony but commonly associated with marriage services 'until death us do part'.

There was a moment of comic relief, Leonard reported, when Vanessa interrupted the registrar to say she had just remembered that she needed to ask how to change the name registered for her two-year-old son from Claudian to Quentin. 'The Registrar stared at her with his mouth open. Then he said severely: "One thing at a time, please, Madam."'

Their first night as a married couple was spent at Asheham. Afterwards, they travelled to Somerset to The Plough in Holford, a sixteenth-century inn at the foot

This portrait of Virginia knitting, in 1912, was one of many portraits painted by her sister, Vanessa.

of the Quantock Hills. The weather was unseasonably wintry and, though they did brave the rain to visit the home of the poet Samuel Taylor Coleridge at Nether Stowey, they spent much of their time hunched over the fire, eating delicious food ('cream for every meal'), reading novels and making plans – 'great fun'.

These plans were focused on where they would live in London: neither Virginia nor Leonard wanted to return to 38 Brunswick Square. They wanted non-commitment, no responsibility, the freedom to rent rooms – 'we expect to be enormously busy, and never to have a real house,' wrote Virginia to a friend. Leonard expressed the expectation that they would live 'a nomadic life . . . I hope when I die like a good Jew at 70 I shall still have no home' (an attitude contradicted by his later opinions). They were united in their reluctance to live in Bloomsbury – at this time they had their eye on the seclusion, the 'otherness', of the lawyers' enclave of the Temple (Clive Bell had had rooms there). But first there would be travels in Europe, a prospect that delighted them both.

There was deep, affectionate attachment between them from the start, Virginia ends a letter one week after the marriage: 'Now I must get my husband to pack my box for me.' (Even at that point, Leonard was in the position of carer.) They left for France in late August, and moved on to Spain and then Italy. Virginia described to Lytton Strachey the way they passed their days – walking in the morning, reading in the afternoon (she read three novels, including *Crime and Punishment* in two days), strolling by the sea in the afternoon and sitting in a café after dinner – and how at night 'the proper business of bed' was interrupted by mosquitos: 'They always choose my left eye, Leonard's right ear.' Though it seems likely that their marriage was never fully consummated, their relationship was close. They talked 'incessantly' for seven weeks.

Back in London, it was not the Temple they moved to but Clifford's Inn, at the end of an alleyway leading from Fleet Street, a part of London that she was attached to all her life. It led through a gatehouse (still there, though the Inn itself was demolished in 1934, and replaced by the current block) to the fourteenth-century building, once an Inn of Chancery providing training for new lawyers. By 1903, this function had ceased, and the buildings were turned into accommodation for a variety of tenants, from painters and photographers to typists and tailors, which

The original gateway to Clifford's Inn, first home of Virginia and Leonard.

provided them both with much interest, but especially Virginia, for whom looking through windows had a lifelong appeal. She often wrote of what she could see while writing letters: 'the gentleman opposite has just got up in his pyjamas and fed his canary while the art student in the garret has got about 20 pigeons sitting on the sill.' Virginia, ever the observer, noted how this young lady flung herself 'in full light, curtains up into a young man's arms the other evening'.

It was all good material for her fiction. Clifford's Inn itself was probably the inspiration for the 'small court of high eighteenth-century houses' where William Rodney in *Night and Day* had his rooms, with its very steep staircase.

She was at the time completing *The Voyage Out*, but the domestic minutiae of her life absorbed her too. Once the chaos of moving in was over, she approved of the arrangements for her new home, with its 'little patch of green for my brats to play in', as well as a porter and bedmaker: pleasingly like a Cambridge college, she thought. The bedmaker was approved of for her broadmindedness. Virginia recounted a conversation with her – 'all this with Leonard naked in his bath – Mrs. W leaning on the W.C. door looking at him'.

Virginia enjoyed the process of setting up home. She added domestic snippets to letters, like this one in May 1913: 'I've got some new curtains and rearranged the room – said to be a great improvement.' A friend, Katherine (Ka) Cox, sent her a set of embroidered drapes, which Virginia at once tried out on a table, sofa and two armchairs to find the best position for displaying. In her thank-you letter to Ka she commented on the joy of 'hearing my rooms praised – very highly, more highly than Nessa's; on account of your present'.

In that same letter she recounts how she came in with six parcels, of 'mutton cutlets, eggs, cake and potatoes'. But she discovered disappointingly that in cooking the cutlets, the outside had a tendency to be done before the inside. This is a rare excursion into catering. The newly married couple took to eating and meeting friends in Ye Olde Cock Tavern, dating from 1547 (the 'Ye Olde' had been added in 1668) in Fleet Street, almost opposite their home. The Cock, which has the narrowest frontage of any pub in London, had a good pedigree – Samuel Johnson and Samuel Pepys had frequented it and Charles Dickens had supped there (and had also written derogatorily about Clifford's Inn in *Our Mutual Friend*, calling it a 'mouldy little plantation or cat-reserve'). It served as the Woolfs' dining room, and Leonard wrote of the pleasure he felt when he was recognized as a regular by the head waiter.

Leonard found Clifford's Inn 'rather beautiful and incredibly ancient' – but also rather draughty and incredibly dirty. Coal fires caused smoke and dust, and there was no relief from it, day or night. If writing near an open window, he found that

Ye Olde Cock Tavern, where Leonard and Virginia frequently dined.

'a thin veil of smuts' covered the paper before he had reached the end of a page.

From their early days they followed the same disciplined working practice they had followed at 38 Brunswick Square: in the morning, each would write, in their separate quarters, at least 500 words (in the early days fiction for both). In the afternoon they might continue writing reviews or essays.

Leonard set about finding freelance work, and took a job as the secretary of Roger Fry's Second Post-Impressionist Exhibition in 1912 at Grafton Galleries (with its catalogue cover designed by Vanessa and Roger and drawn by Duncan), which proved quite as controversial as the first had been: according to Leonard, the pictures caused outrage or laughter. He also took up journalism. He started doing work for the Women's Co-operative Guild, after meeting Margaret Llewelyn Davies, secretary of the Guild. His report of the 1913 Women's Co-operative Guild Congress in Newcastle was published in the *Manchester Guardian* and came to the attention of the social reformers Beatrice and Sidney Webb, leading members of the Fabian Society, the socialist organization that inspired the Labour Party. The Webbs persuaded him to write reports for the society and Leonard became one of the leading political thinkers of the time.

To begin with, Leonard and Virginia split their time between Clifford's Inn and Asheham: though Virginia loved the atmosphere of London, she needed the peace of the countryside, and Asheham was a treasured retreat where they continued the routine of working and reading but adding country walking and gardening.

This cosy and convivial life as they edged their way into comfortable partnership was shattered after the completion of *The Voyage Out*, which was sent to Gerald Duckworth and Company, set up in 1898 by her half-brother. As would happen again and again, the agitation caused by the finishing of a novel brought on a breakdown. From March 1913 onwards, her health began to deteriorate, as she continually suffered with intense worry and insomnia, as well as the savage headaches that betokened much worse. The publication of her novel was deferred for a year.

Though Leonard had known her fragility when he fell in love with her, he cannot have been made aware by Vanessa and Adrian of the extent of her instability, or of her past breakdowns. But with determination and devotion he dealt with this new disturbing state of affairs. He contacted doctors other than Savage, though it seemed to him, probably correctly, that most had little knowledge or understanding of mental illness. It was sometime during the spring that, as her condition worsened, it was decided, in consultation with these doctors and with Vanessa, that it would not be safe for her to have a child. The cradle Violet Dickinson had given as a wedding present would be unused. It was to be a source of pain and regret for both, cropping up intermittently in her diaries, though she later displayed an ambivalent attitude, valuing the creative work that she was aware might have been impossible if they had been parents.

Those last months at Clifford's Inn were overshadowed by anxiety, the sense of promise snuffed out. Leonard described it as a nightmare. Virginia eventually agreed to go to Burley Wood again, from which she wrote sad little letters to Leonard. The plan then, endorsed by doctors, was to return to the Plough Inn in Somerset, but their visit in August went badly as Virginia was refusing to eat and persecuted by imaginings. Leonard had to telegraph Ka Cox for support, and they returned early to London, to the safe haven of 38 Brunswick Square. It was while they were here, however, that as Leonard was, with Vanessa, visiting her doctor he heard from Ka that Virginia was unconscious – she had found Leonard's medical case unlocked, and taken an overdose of Veronal. This was discovered perilously late. Geoffrey Keynes (Maynard's brother, staying in the house), drove Leonard to St Bartholomew's Hospital (where Geoffrey was a surgeon) to fetch a stomach pump. It saved her life.

After that, it was clear that she needed complete and constant care, if she were not to be certified. Leonard indeed visited some nursing homes and dismissed that option as out of the question. But she needed to leave London and stay somewhere big enough for several trained nurses to be in attendance. George Duckworth offered Dalingridge Place in West Sussex, a mansion in enormous grounds with woods, where they spent a few weeks before moving to Asheham in November. It was a fraught time for Leonard.

Alone, he went back to Clifford's Inn in early December and packed up the possessions of their first months together (their combined collections of books were the greatest problem), arranged removal and storage with the firm Joseph May of Howland Street, and left their first home on 5 December.

## MARRIAGE AND PARTNERSHIP – HOGARTH HOUSE

He returned to Asheham, where he cared for Virginia, encouraging her to eat, to drink milk, to rest. By early 1914, the toll was telling on him – he had excruciating headaches himself, and in early March he was compelled to take time off: Ka, Janet Case and Vanessa took turns to be with Virginia and he went to stay with Lytton in a rather comfortless cottage (no sofa and one armchair) in Wiltshire. Lytton was in the process of writing a biographical essay on Cardinal Manning, one of his *Eminent Victorians*, and read portions to Leonard. Despite the extreme situation, he could still write to her from his retreat that there was no doubt that 'we do suit each other in some amazing way. I've never been alone with anyone else for a few days without irritating and being irritated.'

By April, Virginia was sufficiently restored for them to take a holiday in Cornwall, where they visited her old haunts and crept into the garden of Talland House. By the summer, as the world was preparing for war, she seemed well on the way to recovery. A holiday in Northumberland and the Scottish Borders restored her spirits – and her appetite for returning to London, a prospect that filled Leonard with foreboding. They searched in Hampstead, Westminster, Holborn and Chelsea. They also investigated a house in Twickenham when they stayed for a week there at 65 Margaret's Road, and in the end Leonard prevailed upon Virginia to agree to Richmond, far enough away from the excitements that might affect her.

They found a Georgian house that pleased them: Hogarth House was half of a pair, its twin called Suffield House, in Paradise Road. The location was suburban – and there was a mortuary across the road so coffins were a common sight – but there were views over to Kew in the other direction. The rooms were, according to Leonard, 'perfectly proportioned and panelled'; the garden had apple trees. It was not yet available, so in October 1914 they moved into rooms at 17 The Green, ruled over by a Belgian landlady, Mme le Grys. With her good-natured grumbles about her Belgian lodgers – refugees from the war – and their huge Belgian appetites, as well as the antics of the unfortunate maid Lizzie (forever breaking china, or on the verge of setting fire to the house), Virginia found it very entertaining. There were occasional hiccups, as when Virginia tried to cook breakfast from her bed, to Leonard's annoyance. Rows were inevitable with two such strong-minded people, but were quickly resolved, once by Leonard creeping into her bed with the gift of a

This watercolour of 1926 shows 17 The Green, Richmond, where Virginia and Leonard lived for a few months before moving to Hogarth House.

green purse. Though their sexual relationship had faltered, Virginia was tactile: she always liked to be petted, and their conversation and correspondence were full of endearments and animal nicknames. He was Mongoose and she was Mandrill.

Virginia was recovering, and getting used to outer London, though as someone who liked to glimpse other lives by looking through windows, she abhorred what she saw as the suburban tendency of closed windows and closed curtains, but mused on the pride that the residents took in those curtains, singling one set out in particular, of yellow silk striped with lace inserts.

Richmond was close enough to London for Leonard to keep in touch with his burgeoning career as a journalist and his work for the Webbs and the Fabian Society.

## MARRIAGE AND PARTNERSHIP – HOGARTH HOUSE

Leonard and Virginia were invited for a weekend at the Webbs' country house in Surrey where fellow guests were George Bernard Shaw and his wife Charlotte. They found Shaw rather remote to begin with but 'when stirred up he told stories all about himself without stopping'. When he wasn't doing that, he was reading aloud the letters he was writing to the newspapers. In his autobiography, Leonard recounted an occasion much later, in 1933, when he and Virginia met him while walking in Kensington Gardens. Shaw began to tell them about his voyage round the world, discoursing on this for some time. When he finally moved on, Leonard looked around and found fifteen or twenty people gathered listening to Shaw as though it were a performance. Which, as Leonard pointed out, it was.

Virginia was making trips to London to see friends and to attend cookery classes in Victoria where she managed to bake her wedding ring into a suet pudding, but did learn to make omelettes, to Leonard's pleasure. Sometimes she went up to meet Leonard and once she wrote appreciatively of eating a meal at a cabmen's shelter – there were then over sixty of these in London, provided by a fund set up by the Earl of Shaftesbury. (There are still thirteen left.) She visited the London Library (she had a family interest as her father had once been president) or the British Museum. She revered the oak-panelled Reading Room and the 'vast dome, as if one were a thought in the huge bald forehead which is so splendidly encircled by a band of famous names'. Julia Hedge, a character in *Jacob's Room*, wonders why there were no women included.

As negotiations over Hogarth House stumbled, Virginia also made a number of trips to London to investigate other options, revelling in her explorations of Holborn and Bloomsbury again – 'the tumult & riot & busyness of it all'. She went to Gray's Inn to investigate the possibility of renting chambers there: it harked back to their first plan to start married life at Temple, and their tenancy at Clifford's Inn (her friend Ka was now living in the rooms she and Leonard had occupied). She was given a key to a vacant set, experiencing a 'thrill of excitement' as she let herself in. But it was immediately obvious that it was too small for two.

She paid a visit to the Foundling Hospital to ask about the possibility of renting 38 Brunswick Square again – just too late as it was on the verge of being let to a retired Ceylon civil servant. She had an amiable conversation with the hospital's surveyor and estate agent, Mr Chubb, about Duncan's frescoes in Adrian's sitting room (the new tenant planned to cover up the naked tennis players with a curtain). She and Leonard even went to Wimbledon, 'a dreary, high, bleak, windy suburb', to look at a house recommended by Dr Savage. As they came home by bus, she noted that the world grew steadily nicer as they came to Richmond. Settlement on Hogarth House continued to elude them, and Virginia feared they might lose it. She always trusted her instinct on houses, repeating her mantra: 'I have a nose for a house, & that was a perfect house, if ever there was one.'

However, by January the lease had been sorted out. On 25 January 1915 she recorded her birthday treat – a trip 'up to town' on a non-stop train (obviously worthy of note), for a – slightly disappointing – visit to the Picture Palace, a cinema in the West End, and to Buszards Tea Room in Oxford Street. That was much more fruitful, as they discussed their new home, 'far the nicest house in England,' as she wrote to Margaret Llewelyn Davies.

Hogarth House, a Georgian house on Paradise Road, had attracted them immediately on their arrival in Richmond. They lived here for nine years.

Just as exciting was their plan to buy a printing press. They had seen one in Farringdon Road. Leonard wanted to find a physical occupation for Virginia – a manual activity, he felt, would help soothe her mind when it was troubled and be a significant step for her stability. And it would be a joint project. But it was a project deferred – by mid-February she was again seriously ill, perhaps brought on by anxiety over the impending publication of *The Voyage Out*. The financial exigencies of the situation were such that Leonard had to write to Virginia's brother-in-law Jack Hills, widower of Virginia's half-sister Stella, to ask for Virginia's portion of the income from the marriage settlement that he had transferred back to the Stephen family after Stella's death to be brought forward to assist with the cost of nurses. The expenses of the last year had been great and their situation was precarious. Virginia had had to sell some of her jewellery and there needed to be constant financial manoeuvring.

Leonard in Cornwall with Margaret Llewelyn Davies, secretary of the Women's Co-operative Guild, a close friend and colleague.

Virginia descended into a mania of talking constantly and incoherently, and sleeping very little for three days at a time. It was as well that they were moving from the lodgings of Mme le Grys, sympathetic though she was. On 25 March, the day before the publication of *The Voyage Out*, she was taken to a nursing home for a week while Leonard made the move into Hogarth House on his own. So he alone settled into the house that they had both been anticipating with pleasure.

Leonard was smitten with Hogarth House. He had felt, from their first viewing, that the panelled rooms 'even when we first saw them in the dirty dusty desolation of an empty house had beauty, repose, peace, and yet life'. Perhaps, he mused, the people who had built and lived in the house had left the aura of their lives, imposing their personality on the rooms, as though it were a work of art. More prosaically, this was a matter of bricks, mortar and wood – but the way they had been used gave the house its extraordinary character of being 'the perfect envelope for everyday life'.

Leonard had the most fervent belief in the importance of houses. In his autobiography, he considered that they had 'the deepest and most permanent effect upon oneself and one's way of living', providing 'the framework of what one does, of what one can do, and of one's relations with people'. In his perception, the Leonard and Virginia who lived in Hogarth House from 1915 to 1924 were not the same people who lived in 52 Tavistock Square from 1924 to 1939. The Leonard and Virginia who lived in Asheham House from 1912 to 1919 were not the same people who lived in Monk's House from 1919 to 1941. 'In each case, the most powerful moulder of them and their lives was the house in which they lived.'

The interior of Hogarth House, which inspired such musings, was, Leonard felt, full of elegance from the fine staircase to the drawing room with its 'tremendous solidity. . . and yet nothing could have been more light and graceful, more delicately and beautifully proportioned' than the room itself, with its fireplace and great windows, panelling and carved woodwork.

It must have seemed the perfect place for recuperation, but, as Leonard described in *Beginning Again*, the first fortnight when Virginia was home was terrifying, as she slipped into acute illness again, refusing to eat, violent with her nurses, talking incoherently and hallucinating. She turned against Leonard, and Vanessa too. It was two months before she would see him.

When she began to recover, Leonard instigated a careful regime, vigilant over her eating, and spending a high proportion of their total expenditure on food. By the summer, they were passing a lot of time at Asheham, reading endlessly (including in Latin and French), making blackberry jam and collecting mushrooms. By this time Virginia had only one nurse (who supervised her letter-writing – ensuring she did not spend too long on her correspondence).

By the end of November, she was back at Hogarth House and the last nurse was gone, to her relief: no longer did she have to play cards every evening with her. Her attention was turning to a few alterations to the house, which for the first time she could enjoy. The drawing room was carpeted in green – just as at Fitzroy Square.

The plaque on Hogarth House, which marks the founding by Virginia and Leonard of the Hogarth Press.

And she was in search of paint (not always easy to find in the war she noted, because of the shortage of oil, used as a lubricant for guns) and was soon asking Vanessa for proportions to mix paint and size and water, as 'we want to paint the dining room on Sunday'.

She asked Vanessa for advice on arranging the ten tiles they had bought for surrounding the stove like hers in their drawing room. The curtains, possibly bought from the Omega Workshops set up in Fitzroy Square in 1913 by Roger Fry, Vanessa and Duncan, were a great success, conveying the illusion 'that we are grasshoppers sitting on a vine leaf, which was what I wanted'.

Virginia faithfully bought items from the Omega Workshops but one day in 1918 her regret at a purchase of a chair covered in bright yellow checked material drove her almost frantic, and, inspired by a picture of Vanessa's, she went in search of something to cover it, opting first for two pieces of eighteenth-century embroidery, which restored her confidence in her taste, draping them over the chair 'for which I now felt little short of physical rage'. But that did not suit and so she went to Joseph Souhami's, an importer of Oriental textiles, near Oxford Street, and found Persian cloth of pale green and blue on a yellow-white background, which at last obliterated

These items of furniture created by Roger Fry were typical of the Omega Workshops, initiated by Roger in 1913 to produce screens, fabrics, pottery and clothes. Virginia was a supporter.

that 'painful staring check'. Hereafter, she vowed to buy all draperies from him and to avoid Omega.

Virginia wasn't writing again, but she was learning Italian, and later Russian, and as usual reading copiously. She loyally took an interest in the Women's Co-operative Guild, as Leonard was so involved, and joined in activities of the small Richmond branch for four years by organizing monthly meetings and speakers. She also joined the Fabian Society. Leonard, by now editing *International Review* and a regular contributor to the *New Statesman*, also managed to write four books between 1916 and 1920. Virginia told Ka proudly that Leonard had learned to compose straight on to a typewriter: 'I feel like the owner of some marvellous dog that does tricks.' His book *International Government*, which stemmed from a report commissioned by the Webbs and published in 1916, proposed an international agency to enforce world peace, leading almost directly to the League of Nations. He became secretary of two advisory committees of the Labour Party, international and colonial, remaining on them for twenty-seven years.

When conscription in the First World War was introduced in 1916, Leonard was exempted from military service because of the tremor in his left hand that he endured all his life. The war, however, impinged on them, and there were air raids – one night nine bombs dropped on Kew. They spent some nights on mattresses in the kitchen, where Virginia made their servants Nellie Boxall and Lottie Hope giggle, to the annoyance of Leonard, who was trying to sleep. She signed off one letter to Vanessa saying they had eaten most of their dinner in the coal cellar.

Nellie and Lottie, originally Roger Fry's servants, had joined them early that year and were to stay with them for several years, though it was a turbulent relationship. Even in August that year were warning signs of trouble to come when they found Asheham, with its primitive conditions and isolation, too depressing. It was not so surprising as they had been used to Roger's home, Durbins, a new house designed by him, partly open plan and full of light and modern conveniences. By September, however, in the first of many fluctuations in their relationship, they were both anxious to stay on.

It was to be the pattern of their life with servants. Nellie and Lottie would give in their notice. Then they'd recant. 'The vagaries of domestics are quite unintelligible,' was Virginia's verdict. A lot of Virginia's time was taken up in keeping the peace. She had to mediate between Leonard and Lottie: 'they twit each other about their bad tempers' and Virginia lived in fear of Leonard dismissing Lottie if she went away. Her relations with Nellie were always volatile, oscillating between fervent appreciation and extreme irritation at her changing moods. Domestic help was, however, a necessity. Virginia and Leonard could both on occasion deal with cooking meals for guests when required (providing copy for boasting in letters). But the business of housework was a different matter – though even Virginia was driven to making the beds when both Lottie and Nellie succumbed to German measles.

After two years at Hogarth House there was talk of moving to Maids of Honour

Row in Kew – Leonard was briefly keen as the houses had bigger gardens, and it was quieter. That plan lapsed but she and Leonard shared an interest in house-hunting, sometimes exploring houses they came across, with the vague idea of moving or simply to look. She was always interested in looking at the decoration of a house. Just as she had when she was young, counting the dreadful wallpaper of a cousin's office as worthy of note in her diary, she remained acutely aware – and critical – of the appearance of houses. When walking in Kew Gardens one day in 1916, they met Walter Lamb (once her suitor), now Secretary of the Royal Academy (and who may have been the model for Hugh Whitbread in *Mrs Dalloway*) and he invited them back to his home on Kew Green. She described to Vanessa his 'exquisite' residence where all engravings of the eighteenth-century buildings hung perfectly straight on walls of duck-egg green 'and all his books polished and in order'.

She observed people's homes minutely. For example, when she went to a concert at Shelley House in Chelsea, home of St John Hornby and of his Ashendene Press, which specialized in classics published with fine woodcuts and finely tooled bindings, she described it as a sham eighteenth-century house and remarked on the vast portraits of young girls, the paintings on the panels and the pale green Morris curtains and china pots on little wooden stools, all 'far worse than any plush lodging house'. She was critical too of Ka's flat – Ka was by then married to Will Arnold-Forster – 'acid lemon colours against black curtains, and one white rose against a wall the colour of skim milk.' When she visited the Women's Co-operative Guild's headquarters in Hampstead, she commented on the very dignified old house with its eighteenth-century carvings and panelling.

Much later, when revisiting 46 Gordon Square, which was by then the home of Maynard and Lydia Keynes, she noted the alterations made to Vanessa's scheme – ceiling decorations whitewashed, candelabras imported from Maples in Tottenham Court Road (then 'the largest furniture establishment in the world' – it closed in 1997) and primrose-coloured satin curtains sprinkled with violet wreaths, 'which hang tight and shiny across the windows and are met by a sky blue carpet of the thickest pile'. She always had an appreciation of decor. Even the sight of a window in Oxford Street made her 'build up all the chambers of an imaginary house and furnish the room at one's will with sofa, table, carpet'.

Virginia on a walking holiday in Cornwall in 1916.

However, what turned their attention from houses to business was their purchase of a tabletop printing press in 1917. They had made their first enquiries after a printing press in the spring of 1915, not long after Virginia's thirty-third birthday. In late 1916, with Virginia now fully recovered, they talked about it again, but money was short, partly because of the expenses of her illness, and partly because the income tax refund they received at the end of the year was £15 instead of the £35 they'd hoped for.

A tabletop 'Model' printing press. In 1917 Virginia and Leonard purchased one, on which they printed the first publication of the Hogarth Press, *Two Stories*.

But on 23 March 1917, they went to Farringdon Road to the Excelsior Printing Supply Company to make their purchase. The press finally arrived on 24 April. With great excitement they unpacked it and carried it, with Nellie's help, into the drawing room, placing it on the 'very green' carpet – and found it was broken. They were philosophical about it: the shop would have a spare part, and it would anyway take a long time to sort out the blocks of type. The real challenge, Virginia found, was differentiating between the 'h's and the 'n's. Typesetting became her responsibility – Leonard's tremor made that inevitable – but she also cut covers, printed labels, glued spines and dispatched books.

Their original plan had been to learn how to print at the St Bride Foundation Institute in Fleet Street, but they were ineligible for apprenticeship, and evening classes for enthusiastic amateurs did not exist. So they taught themselves from the sixteen-page booklet provided. As Leonard had planned, it proved the ideal distraction from, and balance to, the intense concentrated creativity that possessed Virginia when composing her novels. The actual physical labour she found 'the most absorbing of all pursuits'; it was hard to tear herself away, and she would work three hours at a stretch. She noted with pride the record time she'd taken to set up a page – one hour and fifteen minutes, and recounted her fleeting alarm, when after two hours' work at the press, Leonard 'heaved a terrific sigh and said "I wish to God we'd never bought the cursed thing!" To my relief, though not surprise, he added, "Because I shall never do anything else".'

The one disadvantage was that the dining room became the headquarters of the press, meaning that 'we don't dine so much as picnic,' as Virginia wrote when inviting people, 'soon it will be in bed with us.' But they found it immensely satisfying. Even the printing of their first flier, done by hand, was thrilling.

To start with, they managed all aspects without help – from the actual printing to bookbinding, advertising, packing and posting. Bookbinding was something that Virginia had done in her youth. In the autumn, Emma Vaughan, a favourite cousin of Virginia's from childhood, and who had shared that nascent interest, offered to contribute her extensive equipment. Violet gave them a reading table, the surface of which could be adjusted into a slope, which Virginia found very useful for arranging the type in a more convenient manner. In June they got another tax refund, a much more generous one, which filled Virginia with ideas of buying another press that would print eight pages at a time 'and then we shall be very professional'.

Three months later came the first fruits of their physical labour – a thirty-two-page pamphlet with a cover of blue and red Japanese paper, the spine of each copy stitched in red thread by Virginia. *Two Stories* – Virginia's 'The Mark on the Wall' and Leonard's 'The Three Jews' – was the first product of the Hogarth Press, and the beginning of a new partnership. Its publication in July 1917 was small – just 134 copies were sold. Lytton was particularly complimentary about 'The Mark on the Wall', calling it in a letter to Leonard 'a work of genius. The liquidity of the

Katherine Mansfield, dazzling writer of short stories, was the author of Hogarth Press's second book, *Prelude*, published in 1918.

style fills me with envy: really some of those sentences! – How on earth does she make the English language float and float?'

It was a promising beginning for the dining-room publisher and their afternoons were no longer devoted entirely to walking but to printing. The practical business of setting the type, stitching the papers – even packing the parcels – appealed to Virginia, and it provided a useful outlet for her writing. The first press soon became inadequate, as she wrote in her diary of November 1917, and they obtained a larger one. That in turn was replaced in 1921 by a secondhand Minerva platen press, worked by a treadle.

They set about finding new talent, fixing on Katherine Mansfield's *Prelude*. It also represented a significant stage in her relationship with Katherine, by whom Virginia was half charmed and half repelled. They had a wary friendship, bonded by intense discussions about writing but coloured by Virginia's feeling of rivalry with this younger New Zealand writer. Her early death, in 1923, led to much soul-searching about the loss.

The publication of *Prelude* in 1918 marked a trend towards what would become an extraordinary range of talent for a tiny publisher. T.S. Eliot was one of their earliest authors – it was here in Richmond where Virginia set the type for his *Poems* in 1919, and then *The Waste Land* in 1922. Tom Eliot was 'a strange young man' with a ponderous way of speaking. He became a friend.

They were offered James Joyce's *Ulysses*, which they turned down, partly because it was too big a project, but mainly because the two printers they showed it to pointed out they would be prosecuted for obscenity. It's possible too that Virginia might have felt qualms about publishing it as the style so crept towards her own – though she was also squeamish about the language and patronising about the author.

They studied Russian so they could work with their friend S. S. ('Kot') Koteliansky on translations of Tolstoy and Chekhov. Altogether, it was the beginning of a most productive time for Virginia. *The Voyage Out*, published in 1915 at a time when Virginia was lost in illness, had garnered favourable reviews. Her second (and longest) novel, *Night and Day*, came out in 1919. She made up *Jacob's Room*, published in 1922, while looking into the fire at Hogarth House. This was the book that seemed like a breakthrough, as she felt she was speaking in her 'own voice'. And she was writing several short stories and essays, including *Kew Gardens*, which turned out to be a turning point, in two different ways.

She had begun a collaboration with Vanessa, who designed several of the covers: it was a way of complementing their different skills, a declaration of mutual support – and a resolution of sibling rivalry. But Vanessa was annoyed about the presentation of her woodcuts for *Kew Gardens* and Virginia's visit to her at Charleston in May 1919 failed to assuage her. As a result of her unsettled state, and feeling the need to assert herself in some way, Virginia made an impulse purchase of a house in Lewes that led to their attending the auction of Monk's House in Rodmell. That changed the course of their life.

The other impact was from the success of *Kew Gardens*. Orders flooded in. It was the moment when the hobby press became a proper publisher. There were a frantic few days of cutting, gluing and binding. They decided to reprint 'Mark on the Wall'. Leonard went out and spent 10/6d on a brass nameplate for the door: Hogarth Press.

Assistance was needed – and an ever-changing cast of characters stepped in, from Ralph Partridge (a friend of Lytton's) onwards. At different times there were plans for a bookshop, and even later a shop/tearoom/gallery in Bond Street. Marjorie Joad was enlisted when Virginia, ever attentive to people around, had overheard a conversation at the 1917 Club in Gerrard Street, the meeting place for socialists co-founded by Leonard (and which remained until 1932). Hearing a young woman say she was tired of teaching and wanted to become a printer, Virginia had followed her into the writing room to offer her a job – and thereafter gained wondering insight

T.S. Eliot with Virginia and his wife Vivienne. Tom Eliot was an early contributor to Hogarth Press with his *Poems* in 1919. and *The Waste Land* in 1922, and became a close friend.

into a lower-class world as they lunched together on work days. (She marvelled at someone having a mother who lived in Harpenden.)

In 1920 the owner of Hogarth House refused to renew the lease but then offered to sell it and the other half of the Georgian mansion, Suffield House, to them for £2,000. They bought it – and found six months later that they had to fork out a fortune for repairing the drains. They thought briefly that they might restore the two houses to their original condition and unite them as one. But that was too big a job, and anyway Virginia was already becoming restive in Richmond.

By 1923, she was chafing at the bit. She had begun writing *The Hours*, later *Mrs Dalloway,* which, with its exquisite evocation of peripatetic London, tantalized her and she longed to be back in the thick of it. Even as she wrote of the delight in walking along Bond Street and Piccadilly, and the thrill Mrs Dalloway's daughter Elizabeth found in boarding a bus along the Strand, a feeling so familiar to Virginia herself, she pined for total immersion in her town, rather than living on the outskirts.

The quiet pleasures of Richmond had begun to pall. She was increasingly irritated by excursions to London being curtailed by the last train home, as demonstrated by a letter to Maynard, asking him to send her his latest contribution to the Memoir Club (which had been set up in 1920) as she and Leonard had to leave in the middle of his reading. She wrote of 'the labour of going to London'. Vanessa's children were growing up and 'I can't have them to tea, or go to the Zoo.' By June 1923 she was in a frenzy of frustration that she might have to face 'a life spent, mute & mitigated, in the suburbs' when in London she could go into a concert, the British Museum, a gallery 'or go adventuring among human beings'. She missed riding on the top decks of buses.

She conducted a campaign to convince Leonard to move back to London: it would be a convenient move for him as he was now literary editor of the *Nation* and spending half the week at the office. His anxieties were acute, but at the end of 1923 he capitulated and Virginia began to house-hunt. In early November, she thought she had found her ideal residence at 35 Woburn Square and indulged in flights of fancy about the possibilities of walking her streets again. She was 'filled with joy' as she went past 'our' house with its green doors, opposite the mews, planning the disposition of rooms and occupants. She was, she said, 'heartless about poor old Hogarth where for 9 years we have been so secure.'

Woburn Square came to nothing, but after Christmas she returned to spirited house-hunting, full of plans and energy. She had investigated Chelsea, Maida Vale, Battersea. After Christmas, she planned to restart on Friday 4 January. She was in London again the following Monday when her 'good genius for houses' was aroused on leaving J. W. Coade Son & Budgen, estate agents on Southampton Row, when 52 Tavistock Square was mentioned to her, almost in passing. On her way there she ran into Adrian (he and his wife Karin were living in Gordon Square) and they went together to the offices of Dollman and Pritchard's, the solicitors who were on the ground floor. They went through great green baize doors up to the flat above and then down into the basement where she lost count of the rooms but had decided almost instantly that 'this is our place if ever there was one'.

There were snags, such as the Bedford Estate retaining the right to refuse permission to sublet, but though Leonard was cast down by this, Virginia remained resolute. She was the leader in this enterprise, though she suffered much self-examination in the light of Leonard's reluctance. She couldn't think of work during this domestic matter of such moment. It was nail-bitingly close: the casualness of the solicitor acting for them might have lost it, had Virginia not gone into Coade's, discovered a discrepancy in payment to them, paid it herself there and then and instructed her solicitor from the estate agent's office: 'My house-finding genius was outraged.' She was indeed in control.

Six days later, they had the ten-year lease on 52 Tavistock Square, and she was listing its virtues: basement for the press, a billiard room and rock garden on top, but reserving her greatest excitement for the fact of London, the whole of London, on the doorstep, with its music, talk, friendship, city views, 'all this now within my reach, as it hasn't been since August 1913.' This was a very different Virginia returning to her spiritual home, full of forcefulness and determination.

After arranging for Hogarth House to be leased to the mother of Saxon Sydney-Turner, there were some regrets about leaving – especially for Leonard. Virginia too saw everything through a nostalgic tinge, as she walked by the river, searching for words to describe the willows 'soft yellow plumy, like a cloud. . . something showery in it; and also grains of gold', reflecting that she wouldn't be walking there next spring, though she added 'I am not sentimental about it.' Her view here was of the pagoda in Kew Gardens, but she preferred the 'pale tower' of the Greek Revival St Pancras Church one Euston Road (the three-tier steeple is modelled on Athens' Tower of the Winds), and the view of the red brick and terracotta of the hotels in Russell Square. The Imperial was demolished in 1966 and replaced with what John Betjeman called 'three-dimensional chartered accountancy'. But the Russell Hotel (though in 2018 misguidedly renamed the Principal) remains in all its dusky pink splendour. She revelled in the fact that at long last 'I will have a room of my own to sit down in, after almost 10 years, London.'

But there was little time to ponder as they measured rooms, met builders, arranged cleaning and painting, as well as connecting the utilities. Joseph May, the firm who had removed their furniture and belongings from Clifford's Inn in 1913, was engaged for a fee of £15 to return their furniture and belongings to London, to 52 Tavistock Square.

The day before she left, though rejoicing at abandoning the train journey to London, she paid her respects to this 'beautiful & loveable house, which has done us such a good turn for almost precisely nine years'. On 13 March 1924 the Woolfs moved back into the heart of London.

# A Haunted House
# – Asheham House

*'The flawless beauty of Asheham'*

---

'A Haunted House' is a story about Asheham House in Sussex, in which a benign, ghostly couple revisiting the house is half-sensed by the couple living there. It is short – just a couple of pages – but it is deeply atmospheric, reflecting Virginia's feelings about the spiritual nature of the building. '"Safe, safe, safe," the pulse of the house beat softly.' Leonard felt the same – he sometimes heard noises as if people were walking, sighing, whispering. 'I have never known a house which had such a strong character, personality of its own – romantic, gentle, melancholy, lovely.'

One of the things Virginia and Leonard had shared at the beginning of their relationship was their love of Sussex. What cemented it was their profound feelings about the importance of houses. Leonard Woolf wrote in his autobiography: 'What has the deepest and most permanent effect upon oneself and one's way of living is the house in which one lives.' And it was evident that Asheham held a particular place in their hearts. Leonard described their first sight of it when on a walk: 'In one of those lovely folds or hollows in the down we came upon an extraordinarily romantic looking house.' It became Virginia and Leonard's home from home. Throughout the early years of their marriage, their invaluable refuge was Asheham.

Virginia had first come to know Sussex after the Christmas she and Adrian had spent in Lewes, at the Pelham Arms on the High Street, in 1910. The weather was good and they walked on the Downs on Christmas Day. She was instantly attracted

Asheham, the Regency house discovered by Virginia and Leonard, was their precious retreat between 1912 and 1919.

and began to explore, mindful of advice by doctors and friends to find somewhere she could find rest and respite. On New Year's Day, as she was sitting by the inn's fire, she wrote to Lady Ottoline Morrell that she was tempted to buy a home in the country – though she was thinking more in terms of an eighteenth-century cottage, or even something grander, with oak panelling and marble mantelpieces, rather than a suburban semi.

But a few days later that was what she was in possession of – a newly built semi-detached house with a gable and bay windows, a bathroom, a small garden with a gooseberry bush and what might be currant bushes, she thought. She called it Little Talland House, in memory of her childhood summers – though certainly not in recognition of its appearance: an eyesore, she told friends, 'inconceivably ugly'. The important thing was that it was big enough for guests – she could put up six – and for servants too. It was serviceable rather than charming, but it was in the pretty village of Firle, perfectly situated in the Sussex Downs.

With Vanessa's help she threw herself into the business of making a home. She wrote to Violet of the excitement of furnishing her house and 'staining the floors the colours of the Atlantic in a storm'. Her enthusiasm was such that she started issuing invitations – which meant moving beds around in haste, as well as making curtains and chair covers. Vanessa brought a sewing machine to Firle for the sitting room curtains, which were, according to her direction, to be made of 'bright reddish orange stuff. . . lined and bordered with mauve'. Sophie and Maud, Virginia's cook and housemaid, were the ones to actually make them; Virginia talked of them happily chatting while sewing in the dining room. Little Talland House might have been unattractive, but it was 'done up in patches of post-impressionist colour'.

Her life was pleasantly domestic for a while. She began to do a little catering for herself, and was rather pleased with the results. She tried her hand at hare soup. Meals, she found, took only ten minutes to prepare 'if one is sagacious enough' to think ahead. Owing to this foresight she had 'a potatoe so cooked that its skin rose in cracking bubbles, on the surface, and it was soft to the heart. Also a tapioca pudding.'

This calming time was interrupted in April when Vanessa, on a trip to Turkey, had a miscarriage and a breakdown: Vanessa too was prone to depression. Virginia, as she could, rose to the occasion, going out to tend to her and to help bring her home and, in a reversal of the usual state of affairs, sent cheering letters when she was back at Firle.

Virginia spent a lot of time there this year, alone or with friends including Rupert Brooke (she paid a return visit to the Old Vicarage in Grantchester that August). In July 1911 she invited Leonard for a September weekend, and, when confirming his visit to her country home in August (still addressing him as Mr Woolf), warned him that it was a hideous suburban villa: 'I have to prepare people for the shock.' He arrived late Saturday morning on 16 September, several hours before the other visitors, and she took him straight out on a ten-mile walk. He wrote cryptically in his diary (the very opposite of Virginia's journal) that they had walked to Alfriston, had tea and talked until the early hours. The following day, they were reading companionably together in Firle Park. It was a weekend that set the tone for their relationship that led to their marriage in 1912.

Little Talland House, on the left, was Virginia's first Sussex home, in Firle, a village close to the Sussex Downs.

It must also have been that same September weekend that they came across Asheham House, tucked away in beech woods beneath the rise of Iford Hill with a field of sheep in front, as the following month Virginia was writing to him about her spirited discussion with the owner about water closets and earth closets – and asking Leonard's advice. Built in 1820, as a country retreat for a Lewes solicitor, Asheham was a charming Regency house, single-storey pavilions flanking each side. There were two large sitting rooms, four main bedrooms on the first floor, with servants' rooms and a spacious attic in the roof. French windows led on to a red-tiled terrace, and the view was across the Ouse valley to Rodmell. It beguiled her in a way that Little Talland House could not. That autumn, she and Vanessa signed the lease, and she transferred the tenancy of Little Talland House to Robin Mayor, fellow of King's College, Cambridge, and an acquaintance of Leonard's.

Leonard was closely involved in the refurbishment of Asheham, along with Vanessa, Clive and Adrian. He wrote to Virginia about his help in laying the carpets, 'which I hope you note are, thanks to Vanessa, laid most professionally'. In February, the coldest month for 40 years (the pipes were frozen), there were two housewarming parties on successive weekends; first Virginia's, and then the Bells'. Leonard went to both. It was not long before he was spending more time there than Vanessa was, and it was where he and Virginia spent the first night after their marriage.

Their early weekends together at Asheham were conducted in a very orderly manner – as he informed Lytton in early 1913, they each wrote 750 words in the morning, and between tea and dinner 500 words apiece and 'in the afternoon we dig'. The garden was where Leonard began to pursue what became a lifelong passion, planting wallflowers and nasturtiums, as well as vegetables. (Vanessa didn't always approve of their efforts.)

Though this was not a full-time home, Leonard had an urge to buy two cows and 20 hens, so they could have milk, butter and eggs. There was even talk of renting 'a little shooting'. In March 1913, rather surprisingly, Virginia was asking friends about buying two horses, and by May they had a brood mare and a grey pony, on which – for a brief while – they rode on the Downs. She was undeterred even by being thrown one day. The following year Leonard bought Virginia a – rather more manageable – bicycle from the Co-op in Lewes.

These pastoral plans were interrupted by Virginia's breakdown and attempted suicide that summer, but Asheham played a crucial role in her convalescence. They adjourned there in November for almost a year, firstly with a team of nurses. She wrote to Leonard, who was in Clifford's Inn at the beginning of December packing up their possessions, that she and her nurse had been cleaning the drawing room: 'It's really rather fun, and makes a wonderful difference, even in the smell of the air.'

By February 1914, the last nurse had left and she was following doctor's orders: quiet, rest – and a great deal of milk. In June, Leonard was able to leave her alone in Asheham to attend a Women's Co-operative Guild meeting in Birmingham, after drawing up an agreement with her about her activities in his absence: half an hour lying down to rest after lunch, drinking a '<u>whole</u>' glass of milk in the morning, and to be in bed by precisely 10.25 every night. She detailed her searches for milk at farms around. Once, Vanessa was thinking of cycling over with a can of milk round her neck, but eventually Virginia managed to order a quart a day from the dairy at Southease.

Leonard often went swimming at Seaford, a few miles away. It was while he was swimming in the sea on 1 August 1914 that he heard from another bather, a policeman on holiday just recalled to duty in London, that Britain was about to be at war with Germany.

Living in such a remote place during the First World War was labour-intensive. To begin with, labour – and caretaking in their absence – was provided by local wives (in particular, the shepherd's wife, Mrs Funnell), though they were not as amenable as servants. Not that servants were much more amenable: Nellie and Lottie, who came to Asheham soon after joining the Woolf household from Roger Fry's in 1916, found its primitive conditions little to their liking; Durbins with its labour-saving devices was still fresh in their minds. Here cooking was done by primus and oil lamp, water had to be pumped and carried in buckets, coal and logs to be fetched and earth closets to be emptied into the cesspool. It made the servants unhappy.

Frequent guests included close friends and Hogarth Press authors. One weekend in 1918 Beatrice and Sidney Webb visited, when there was 'incessant talk for 48

Beatrice and Sidney Webb, founders of the Fabian Society, who commissioned reports from Leonard, which led to his lifelong involvement with the Labour Party.

hours'. During the privations towards the end of the war, Virginia was requesting visitors to bring butter, 'far the most precious thing in the world here', as the Co-op would only give two ounces a week, which 'merely greases the top of one's toast at breakfast', leaving dry bread for tea. There was foraging: they picked mushrooms almost every day in late summer, gathered blackberries for jam, and they roasted apples.

The pleasantest times seem to have been when they were alone there. There was much reading (Leonard made bookcases) and also cooking: Virginia asked Vanessa for advice on cheap dishes to cook and perfected her bread-making skills. Before long was making rolls: not as good as Vanessa's but better than Nellie's. She became so adept at making bread – and cakes – that she was able to send presents over to Vanessa, and boasted of making 'really expert bread'. She continued with her bread-making through her life – though it did get in the way sometimes: she once complained that making bread and buns ruined her morning's work because of her repeated visits to the kitchen.

Even the setbacks were enjoyable when faced together, such as the storm one night in April 1917 when they were in bed, when trees were blown over, smashing the terrace: Virginia contrasted the violence of the weather outside with their cosiness inside the bedroom. The next day Leonard cut up the trees into logs, and Virginia noted the delicious smell of the wood fires. Other mishaps included a 'nursery' for swallows in the earth closet and a swarm of bees that got down the chimney into the attic (they shut the door and left them swarming in the grate).

She kept a diary there, with very brief entries: notes of foraging for mushrooms and milk, planting of nasturtium seeds in the walled garden, the trouble in travelling one July because of crowded trains, and how at Christmas in 1917 they made do with a chicken as turkey was too expensive. There were notes on the

Charleston Farmhouse was discovered by Leonard and Virginia, who persuaded Vanessa to rent it.

German prisoners of war at work in the ditches, or bringing in the harvest.

Just as Virginia and Leonard had found Asheham, it was they, appropriately enough, who were responsible for Charleston, which was to become so associated with Vanessa. It was Leonard who actually saw it first in May 1916, taking a photograph with his Kodak camera, and Virginia urged Vanessa to take the farmhouse, extolling its virtues – pond, fruit trees, large rooms, one very suitable for a studio with big windows. Leonard thought it almost as nice as Asheham – though they agreed the wallpaper was dreadful. By September, Vanessa was on the verge of negotiating; Virginia was sure that 'if you get Charleston, you'll end by buying it forever.' As it turned out.

Vanessa, her two children along with Duncan and his lover David Garnett, and occasionally Clive (Vanessa and he were still married and companionable) were ensconced by the end of the year and the wallpaper was soon covered with 'various bright shades of Distemper'. It became Vanessa's masterpiece. Virginia wrote to Violet about Vanessa's 'astonishing' ménage – hares, children, gardeners, ducks, hens and 'painting all the time, 'till every inch of the house is a different colour'.

Interaction between the two households was frequent. Vanessa's sons, Julian and Quentin, came to stay often. One such time was just after the birth of Vanessa's third child (a daughter fathered by Duncan, though it was eighteen years before she was told that) on Christmas Day in 1918.

Quentin (left) and Julian, sons of Vanessa and Clive Bell and frequent visitors to Virginia's homes.

For weeks afterwards, Virginia's letters were full of lists of names, from Clarissa to Griselda. 'Leonard wants you to call her Fuschia; that is his favourite name, and he long ago decided to call his daughter that.' When Vanessa decided on Angelica in March, Virginia was delighted, saying she was just on the point of wiring her to suggest that name, a name with 'liquidity and music, a hint of green in it'.

It was about this time that their comfortable existence at Asheham came to an end when the landowner Mr Hoper gave notice that it would be needed the following year for his farm bailiff, Frank Gunn. It was a grievous blow. They plunged into anxious activity. Leonard went off on his bicycle to scout the area and came back with news of an old manor house at Denton, which sounded promising until they actually visited it.

They investigated a plot of land in a hamlet a mile away with the idea of building, wrote to Robin Mayor to find the availability of Little Talland House at Firle (a poor substitute now for Asheham) and – in a panic that was more informed by nostalgia than practicality – bought leases on three cottages at the hamlet of Higher Tregerthen, near St Ives. These were the ones that had been rented by D.H Lawrence and his wife Frieda, and also briefly by Katherine Mansfield. Lawrence wrote to Leonard describing them: 'on a hillside slap above the sea, which is about ten minutes, down the fields. It is beautiful, I think, and as lonely as necessary.' But it was too distant for a weekend retreat.

Then, one hot summer's day, Virginia, who was upset after an argument with Vanessa over the presentation of her woodcuts in *Kew Gardens*, went on to Lewes to look at a house for sale that Leonard had suggested – and which she thought was like a Surrey mansion. With time to spare before her train back to London, she visited the estate agent Wycherley's on the High Street, which is still in business now. (The website says 'A member of this Wycherley family has sold and rented houses, shops and just about anything in Lewes and the surrounding villages, since 1853.')

Mrs Wycherley told her about a house but thought it a little modest for someone who had lived in a house such as Asheham. However, Virginia went to see the Round House at the top of Pipe's Passage – round because it was the base of a windmill, the upper part having been lopped off. Its quirkiness, the view over the

*Kew Gardens,* with its cover by Roger Fry, was Virginia's second book for Hogarth Press, and changed its fortunes.

town, the sense of isolation on the hill though all around was urban – along with a sense of urgency over finding a replacement for Asheham – propelled her decision. And it was cheap, just £300 for the freehold. She bought it, in a mood of defiance. (She later blamed Vanessa's 'severity' over *Kew Gardens* for her impulse buy.)

When Virginia brought Leonard to inspect it at the end of June, they saw a notice on their way from the station – Monk's House, Rodmell, with three-quarters of an acre of land, to be auctioned the following Tuesday: Leonard murmured 'a house that would have suited us exactly.' It was a house they already knew: they had often walked to Rodmell over the water meadows by the River Ouse. Rodmell was basically one street of cottages formed by chalk-bound flint walls, with a general store, a pub, a forge, a post office and a twelfth-century church. From the path to the church, they had peered over the wall into the garden of Monk's House, and hankered after the orchard.

They visited the Round House without enthusiasm – Leonard was not taken with the cramped little dwelling squeezed into the top of a steep alley – and by then perhaps she was not either. The following day Virginia cycled over to see Monk's House, 'an unpretending house, long and low', brick and flint with white weatherboarding and a steep, tiled roof, and wrote in her diary of how she tried to put herself off by reciting to herself the disadvantages – the small rooms, the inadequacy of the kitchen, the lack of bath and hot water – but she was attracted by the unexpected flowers blooming among the cabbages, the neat rows of vegetables, 'an infinity' of fruit trees, 'the plums crowded so as to weigh the tip of the branch down.' And she mused on the vista of the orchard 'with the grey extinguisher of the church steeple pointing my boundary.'

The Round House in Lewes (opposite) was an impulse buy for Virginia in May 1919, and sold two months later. The plaques detail her initial pleasure in this house with its quirky rooms and view across the town.

So within the space of a paragraph, she had moved from criticism to describing it as 'my' boundary. And when Leonard came to look at it he too was enthused, especially by the garden (Virginia said even then that he had the making of a 'fanatical lover' of that garden) and by all its outhouses, including stable and henhouse, one shed crammed with oak beams, another with pea props.

On 1 July 1919, they went to the auction at the White Hart Hotel, commissioning Mr Wycherley to bid up to £800. Virginia anxiously scanned the crowd for possible rivals, and endured the agony of seeing that there were several interested parties before they made the successful bid, obtaining it for £700. For just over a fortnight they were the owners of two houses in Sussex: on 16 July, they sold the Round House – at least there was a profit of £20.

Their farewell dinner party on 24 August for several friends, including the Bells, Duncan Grant, Maynard Keynes and Morgan Forster, was tinged with sadness. They regretted losing the 'flawless beauty' of Asheham: twenty years later, Virginia still remembered sitting in the garden 'so sublime'. She was intent to the last on soaking up the atmosphere of this very precious house. 'How happy we've been at Asheham! It was a most melodious time.'

Five years later they were offered the chance to buy Asheham, but refused. Had they realized that a cement company was going to buy it and ruin their future view from Monk's House forever, they might have thought differently.

## A HAUNTED HOUSE – ASHEHAM HOUSE

Monk's House in Rodmell, which they already knew from their walks in Sussex, was bought by the Woolfs at auction in Lewes in July 1919.

# London Renewed – 52 Tavistock Square

## *'To walk alone through London is the greatest rest'*

'Life, London, this moment in June': Clarissa Dalloway's joy in her walk to buy flowers, making her way from Westminster across St James's Park to Piccadilly, where she looked for the china cockatoo in the window of Baroness Burdett's home (where Charles Dickens had delightedly provided interior décor advice) and made a brief detour to Hatchard's bookshop before arriving at the florist in Bond Street, mirrors Virginia's own delight in her familiar surroundings. She had begun to write her quintessential London novel *Mrs Dalloway* while living in Richmond and longing for London, and the city provided the setting and the scenes for many of her novels, such as *Jacob's Room* and *The Years. Night and Day* is set entirely in 'the wonderful maze of London', while *Orlando* makes use of its history, vividly evoking the Greenwich home of the English court during the Great Frost. The spires of the City churches she loved found their way into much of her text. In a lyrical paragraph of London at night in *Orlando*: 'As the sun sank, all the domes, spires, turrets, and pinnacles of London rose in inky blackness against the furious red sunset cloud.' And similarly in *The Years:* 'And from all the spires of all the London churches – the fashionable saints of Mayfair, the dowdy saints of Kensington, the hoary saints of the city – the hour was proclaimed.'

After her reclusive existence in Richmond, it was bliss to be back herself, 'right in the centre and swim of things'. London was now on her doorstep; she had the streets to stride along, the squares to sit and ponder in, the British Museum

Virginia in a portrait taken for *Vogue* magazine in 1925.

Reading Room at hand, concerts close by, and (though she affected to care little about her clothes) a dressmaker in nearby Judd Street.

For Leonard, the pleasure was mixed. It was more efficient to be nearer his places of work, and for his political interests. The siting of the Hogarth Press, increasingly important in their lives, was more convenient. But he had loved Hogarth House, and would occasionally return. Of course, there was a practical reason for that, as the house still belonged to them, but after Mrs Sydney-Turner's death two years later, Hogarth House was sold (in 1927) and he went with his sister Flora to bid a formal goodbye to their home for nine years. He returned once more in the 1930s – to find, shockingly, that it was the local branch of Oswald Mosley's British Union of Fascists.

Virginia, fond though she had been of Hogarth House (52 Tavistock Square could not match it for grace and style), liked the low-key elegance and the central location of their new home. And it was a well-constructed house – built in the early nineteenth century, with four storeys and a basement protected by wrought iron railings – that fitted into the London terrace with dignity.

Tavistock Square was part of the Bedford Estate, which was originally laid out in the eighteenth century. The name derives from the courtesy title Marquess of Tavistock, given to the eldest son of the Duke of Bedford, just as Gordon Square is named after the 6th Duke of Bedford's wife, Georgiana Gordon. Bedford Estates is still the largest private landowner in Bloomsbury, and, with good building and garden squares at the heart of the enterprise, has been regarded as 'the best managed urban estate in England'.

Its roots go back to 1669, when William, the son of the 5th Earl of Bedford married Rachel, the daughter of the 4th Earl of Southampton, who had recently inherited from her father an area of agricultural fields, with some development already begun. Individual houses and streets were added intermittently, but it was not until the 6th Duke of Bedford that more considered change was made.

In the 1820s, he commissioned Thomas Cubitt, at the beginning of his career, to develop the pastures into Tavistock Square. Cubitt was a leading master builder whose impact on London can be seen in areas from Belgravia to Clapham, but especially in Bloomsbury – his squares provided the architectural

Thomas Cubitt, master builder who designed many of the Bloomsbury squares before moving on to Belgravia and Pimlico.

backdrop to the Bloomsbury Group. 'Bloomsbury squares always intoxicate me with their beauty,' Virginia wrote shortly after her return to London. Cubitt's different techniques can still be seen in Frederick Street, close to his workshop on Gray's Inn Road: he took care to design the brick and stucco houses in batches of different styles (elaborately roofed balconies on some, with open ironwork and pilasters). It served as a pattern book for potential clients – one of whom was Queen Victoria: Cubitt left his mark on Buckingham Palace as well as Osborne House, her retreat on the Isle of Wight. It was Cubitt's firm who installed the soundproof study at the top of Carlyle's house in Chelsea, recorded by Virginia after she visited with her father in 1897. One of his last jobs was for Charles Dickens, creating extensions and alterations to Tavistock House, on the

The south side of Tavistock Square in the 1930s. The Woolfs lived at 52, in the centre of the terrace. The Hogarth Press was in the basement.

east side of the square, much commended by visitors to the house for its 'bright airy interiors'. Demolished in 1901, it was replaced by a building designed by Edwin Lutyens for the Theosophical Association, and is now the headquarters of the British Medical Association.

   The ground and first floor of 52 Tavistock Square were the offices of solicitors Dollman and Pritchard, described by Leonard as Dickensian. The head of the firm, George Pritchard, became a good friend. The top two floors were Virginia and Leonard's home. Virginia immediately commissioned painted panels from Vanessa and Duncan for the sitting room, forcing Leonard to agree to the 'outrageous extravagance' of £25. By the autumn, she considered the house 'perfect', inviting friends to view the 'moonrises and prima donna's bouquets'.

There had been the tiresome business attendant on any move: 'trying to hook together all the resources of civilisation', as Virginia put it, of telephone, gas and electric light. She felt 'jangled and splintered' by the upheaval: she claimed not to have a single book left whole. There were negotiations with the servants. Nellie, despite her considerable objections (a pattern of life for the next decade), decided to stay with them, while Lottie transferred to the Gordon Square home of Virginia's brother Adrian and his wife Karin.

There were other teething problems. The noise was one. Virginia, fearful that she could not sleep in the flat after the tranquillity of Richmond, put her bed in a small room at the back of the basement, but rats scampering round her bed quickly put an end to that plan. The rats had come from a building site at the back of the house on Woburn Place, eventually to be the Royal Hotel, and caused much disturbance during its construction. Even more disturbance came later from the jazz band in its ballroom, which led to a successful campaign and court case by Leonard against the owners.

The panels, painted by Vanessa Bell and Duncan Grant, were commissioned by Virginia for 52 Tavistock Square.

The Hogarth Press, by now a thriving business, took up residence in the basement. The office was in what was the kitchen, its dresser and range still in place, and a schoolmaster's desk served as the counter. In the scullery was the printing press, where Virginia spent part of her time setting type for the small books of poetry that they still produced here. (In 1927 Dorothy Wellesley, herself a poet and extremely wealthy, sponsored the series *Hogarth Living Poets*.) By then most of the books were printed elsewhere.

What was the butler's pantry next to the kitchen, with its capacious cupboards, became the premises of the manager – of whom there were many. Marjorie Joad had to leave in 1925 because of ill health; Dadie Rylands, Angus Davidson and Winifred Holtby all served time there. John Lehmann worked there from 1931–32, and then returned in 1937 as a partner.

Managing the Hogarth Press was never going to be easy – for employers or employees. For Virginia and Leonard the Hogarth Press was a part-time occupation, alongside their other commitments. (And their holiday trips often involved visiting bookshops to sell in their titles.) Leonard, who was in charge day-to-day, was literary editor of the *Nation* until 1930; in 1927, after the proud purchase of an Algraphone (the gramophone named for the first letters of its maker Alfred Graham) he also began to review records for the magazine. In 1931 he became co-editor of the *Political Quarterly*, which he had helped establish two years earlier. The first volume of his planned series on the psychology of man as a social animal, *After the Deluge*, was published the same year (though he was deeply disappointed, and Virginia cast down, by its low-key reception) and he was asked by the BBC to give six talks on the Modern State. He was also contributing regularly to the *New Statesman*, as well as working for the Labour Party.

Leonard was a meticulous organizer – he'd learnt that from his time in the Civil Service in Ceylon; he was also exacting. There were, inevitably, disagreements with the staff. He was, however, according to his nephew Cecil Woolf (who was inspired to set up his own publishing house in 1960), 'humane and had good literary judgment, a healthy respect for money and the ability to make crude commercial decisions'.

Virginia was also involved on a daily basis. All her books were published by Hogarth, including *The Voyage Out* and *Night and Day*, when the rights reverted from Duckworth (she was, she said, the only woman in England free to write what she liked), and she was still typesetting, reading incoming manuscripts and meeting prospective authors. She worked at the heart of the enterprise. At the rear

Virginia with John Lehmann, manager of Hogarth Press from 1931–32 and later a partner, sitting by the fishpond at Monk's House.

of the house built over the back yard was a semi-subterranean room, once used for billiards and now the storeroom, full of books at various stages of production, and also boxes and Vanessa's canvases. Windowless but with a large skylight, this was the place Virginia chose to work, according to Leonard, 'embedded among the pyramids and mountains of parcels, books and brown paper', seated in a broken-down armchair by the gas fire, with a board across her knees – in the same manner as her father. She wrote in pen and ink in a notebook that she bound herself in coloured paper. Then in the afternoon she typed at the table, which, with its pile of notebooks, drafts, timesheets and manuscripts, could not be disturbed. Virginia considered the room to be 'the best study I've ever had'. She did make some improvements: on Vanessa's advice she bought matting from Hammonds, a Lewes furniture shop, for £2, to lay down on the floor, later adding rugs.

The basement was busy, with deliveries and dispatches, authors and reps coming and going. Cecil remembers being enlisted as a boy to help with the packing, his hands becoming red and cut from tying up the parcels of books. On occasion, when there was a rush, usually on publication of one of her books, Virginia would join the production line, cutting paper, packing, tying string. Hogarth continued to add impressively to its list: Robert Graves, Edith Sitwell, Cecil Day Lewis and E.M. Forster, as well as other members of the Bloomsbury Group – Roger Fry, Maynard Keynes and Clive Bell. In a nod to her eminent great-aunt, there was also a book of photographs by Julia Margaret Cameron with an introduction by Virginia. In 1924 they took on the International Psycho-Analytical Library, thus becoming the English publishers of the works of Sigmund Freud (whom they later met in 1939 shortly before his death: notably, he presented Virginia with a narcissus). In June that year, Virginia urged Vita Sackville-West, already an established author whom she had first met in 1922, to write a book for the Hogarth Press.

*Seducers in Ecuador*, devised when Vita was on a walking trip in the Dolomites in July 1924, was completed in August, delivered on 13 September, sent to the printers on 15 September and published in November. After Vita's first visit to Monk's House that year, Leonard and Virginia sat by their log fire agreeing about the niceness of Vita – and she was certainly generous, with lifts and gifts. She gave Leonard a spaniel puppy that he firstly named Fanny and later Pinker (or Pinka),

Virginia described Knole, childhood home of Vita Sackville-West, as 'more like a town than a house' with 'all its chimneys smoking busily'.

telling her husband Harold Nicolson 'he *was* pleased, he adores dogs'. Virginia visited her at Long Barn where she noted the opulence – butler, silver, hot water, Persian rugs – but concluded that she preferred her own room in Tavistock Square; it had more life in it, she felt. That same year, Vita took Virginia to Knole, the magnificent mansion that had been her childhood home and that she, as a female, could not inherit. This encounter was to have remarkable results.

In the coming years, there would be times when the Woolfs longed to release themselves from the burden of the Hogarth Press (and buy a cottage in the North, as one brief plan had it). But the Press was doing well: income was so good in 1929 that there were bonuses for the workers. Virginia marvelled at the fact that '7 people depend on us.' In 1930, a new printing press was installed. The old Minerva was given to Vita – who, that year, had produced another bestseller for the Press,

Lady Sybil Colefax, a society hostess known for her good taste, which she used later to set up an interior decorating firm after the Wall Street crash reduced her fortune.

*The Edwardians* – and can still be seen in the library at Sissinghurst Castle. By 1938, their earnings were 'prodigious'. All this, she observed, had sprung from the tabletop press in the dining room at Hogarth House.

Being in the heart of London had made the publishing more efficient; it certainly increased their social life. Virginia had for several years been on Lady Ottoline Morrell's invitation list – it was at one of her parties that she made a new friend, Elizabeth Bowen, over a discussion about ice-creams (Virginia was planning to make gooseberry ice-cream). The publication in 1919 of *Night and Day* had also spurred Lady Sybil Colefax, another society hostess and subsequently (rather to Virginia's surprise) founder of an interior decorating firm, the forerunner of Colefax and Fowler, to issue frequent invitations – which, in years to come, were a mixed blessing to Virginia. The Woolfs had an ever-expanding group of friends, with whom Virginia in particular was making up for lost time.

Virginia was in constant demand as a guest, though she was often in agonies of anxiety over dinner invitations. When she boldly had her hair shingled in 1932, following Vita's example, she said that one of the great advantages was that it had robbed dining out of half its terrors – the fear of her hair coming undone. The other half was perennial worry over her clothes and appearance: she turned to

Dorothy Todd, editor of *Vogue*, for advice and once admitted to a 'great lust for lovely stuffs & shapes', but was always self-conscious.

She was, however, often confident in her skills as raconteur. Her riffs, her expansion of a story or a nugget of information imparted to her by a friend or acquaintance, would turn into an episode of great hilarity, but could also cause great discomfiture for the butt of her humour. Leonard, of course, would often be the object of her banter, but he had a dry wit and skills of his own in repartee.

Such popularity made Leonard's task as Virginia's protector more difficult. Virginia's wholehearted appreciation of the social occasions she could now attend more easily often meant she would overdo it, becoming excited and overstimulated, and she would suffer as a result. Combined with the constantly recurring anxieties about her books, she would frequently fall ill. The chronology appended to Quentin Bell's biography shows that in the year starting January 1925, during which time *Mrs Dalloway* and *The Common Reader*, a collection of her articles for the *Times Literary Supplement*, were published, she was in bed, or out of action for several periods ranging from two weeks to nearly four months.

Interspersed were the lesser phases of the depression, always lurking: she summed up her state vividly as 'a little strip of pavement over an abyss'. Sometimes, horribly, in the middle of the night, she would be struck with the sensation of

Bust of Virginia Woolf erected in Tavistock Square by the Virginia Woolf Society.

waves rising and crashing, when the lack of children made her 'wretched' or she remembered moments of mortification. A recurring theme was jealousy of Vanessa's life – of her painting, of her family, of her self-sufficiency. She made efforts to think positively, listing the pleasures of walking on the Downs, of working when she wished, of her earning power, but the regrets recurred: 'Oh but Nessa has children, Maynard carpets.'

A stray remark would lead her in a moment from confidence in her skills, both as a writer (what she herself calls her 'genius') and socially, as friend and conversationalist, to self-denigration as vain, chattering and inconsequential. She would relive moments of humiliation at being mocked by Clive for a new hat, or for her taste for green paint. 'If it were not for the divine goodness of L. how many times I should be thinking of death,' she observed.

In her more philosophical moments, however, she felt that the depths into which she could sink were in themselves a useful corrective, a time of examining her spirit. She reflected on the 'mystical side of this solitude'. Even the bouts of flu could provide time when enforced idleness was profitable. Sometimes then she felt a sense of creativity, of being super-attuned to the sounds of life. It was not all one way. While Leonard worried about her, his eczema flaring up at times of stress, she also worried about his health. And when he was ill she tended to him, enjoying the reversal of roles.

Leonard was constantly watchful. Virginia herself also had learned to retreat, to rest, when she had warning signs. She would hibernate, drink milk, eat apples. She plotted ways to raise her mood. She kept herself busy to tame her 'squirrel cage mind'. Her work schedule was prodigious and, in between, she read constantly, made tapestries, practised languages. She went back to her Greek and Russian, and learned some Italian for a holiday. She forced herself one year to read only French for a month. She told Violet about the stilted conversations she and Leonard were having in Regent's Park, about limited subjects like the weather and the zoo – stilted because they were practising their French.

And she walked. Though she and Leonard took walks together, catching a train to Epping Forest or Surrey – she more usually went on her own. It was something that, as she realized in a conversation later in life, Leonard had minded and, as a result had cultivated the detachment that probably helped him survive his situation. But for Virginia such solitariness was essential: 'To walk alone in London is the greatest rest.' She had given the same enthusiasm to Rachel in *The Voyage Out*: 'I like walking . . . I like seeing things going on – I love the freedom of it.' And it gave her the chance to glimpse fragments of other people's lives, seeing through windows the 'bright rooms', as was echoed by Clarissa's former suitor Peter Walsh while he walked round London in *Mrs Dalloway*. Life going on in beautiful houses; scenes of brilliancy; to see 'people very clearly outlined' filled her with joy. Clarissa Dalloway looks out of her drawing room and sees an old woman through a lighted window, just

Vanessa Bell's cover for what is known as Virginia's London novel.

as Virginia did when she looked out of her nursery and saw Mrs Redgrave. It's what she did when she lived in Clifford's Inn, at close quarters with other tenants, writing to friends with animation about the tableaux of other people's lives, and transmuting her observations into her fiction.

Walking was her interest and a necessity. Sometimes it was to walk off anger, or to lift her depression; or simply to walk herself 'serene'; sometimes she would walk to talk out a book. Her street sauntering and square haunting, as she called it, took her all over London: through the City, the streets and alleys near Fleet Street, down to Southwark, along the mud beaches of the Thames at low tide, to Wapping Old Stairs, along Oxford Street – describing (in a scene that has changed little) the buses 'strung on a chain. People fight & struggle. Knocking each other off the pavement.' Her essay 'Street Haunting' described the route taken and the

The grave of Virginia's great-grandfather, James Stephen (whose name can just be made out), which she discovered on one of her walks.

episodes noted on an errand to the Strand to buy a pencil. She would walk long distances: she once walked out to Cockfosters in the distant outskirts of north London. In July 1937, she walked to Stoke Newington to St Mary's, an Elizabethan church that she thought looked as if it 'might be in a hollow under the downs'. She was on a family quest to find the fine table grave (now a listed monument, restored in 2008) of her great-grandfather James Stephen, Member of Parliament and anti-slavery campaigner, and once resident of next-door Clissold Park.

Her walks were sometimes random, sometimes programmed; if the latter, the destination ideally had to have an A.B.C. tea room (set up by the Aerated Bread Company, the tea rooms feature in two of her novels, *Night and Day* and *Jacob's Room*). In September 1925, she planned a series of Wednesday walks to Gunnersbury, Kenwood and Greenwich: she took the last of these suddenly one day, in reaction to a regretted decision to accept a dinner invitation followed by sending a telegram to cancel. Deeply unsettled, she shook herself down and set off for Greenwich – and found herself entranced by the ships, the Wren buildings and the coat Nelson wore at Trafalgar. Her self-medication worked.

Closer to hand was Tavistock Square, which they visited daily. Now it is open to visitors but then it was for the exclusive use of residents, and in the charge of a park-keeper, with whom Leonard became friendly. It was not long before he was on the garden committee. As residents, they had a key and Virginia and Leonard would walk round and round to worry about Nellie and her ultimatums, or to sort out problems with the Press – or just to walk the dog. (Occasionally, they would take sherry and glasses in there when they had guests.) In 1933 she wrote a letter to *New Statesman* suggesting that London squares might be opened during the summer to those who didn't have the means to leave town.

It was one day in 1925 in Tavistock Square that she made up *To the Lighthouse* in 'a great, apparently involuntary rush'. By the following February, she was in full flow, writing easily. Inevitably, there were qualms when she'd completed it but Leonard, who was always the first to read her manuscripts, declared it a masterpiece, a 'psychological poem'. Forster was 'inclined to think it is your best work'. The poet Stephen Spender told her later that it was the only novel apart from *War and Peace* that he had read four or five times. Her writing was developing, becoming more distinctive. It proved a turning point for her – both personally, by laying the ghosts of her parents who had dominated her adult life, and professionally, by confirming her position in the literary world, and increasing her social cachet.

One high point was tea in the summer of 1926 with Thomas Hardy, who had been a protégé of her father, Leslie Stephen. Leslie, when editor of *The Cornhill Magazine*, had commissioned *Far from the Madding Crowd*, which became a bestseller and allowed Hardy to leave his job as an architect. The meeting at his Dorset home was both enthralling and intimidating to Virginia who devoted several pages of her diary to it. Not all invitations turned out so well. In March of that year, Virginia had invited novelist Rose Macaulay to dine at Tavistock Square (and bought a bedspread beforehand to cover an ugly chest of drawers). Macaulay reciprocated by inviting them to dinner at a restaurant opposite her flat. Thinking it to be a small, casual affair they arrived late, straight from the Press, with unchanged clothes and inky fingers, to find themselves in the company of several literary personages in all their finery. Leonard's tremor increased, as was common when he was discomfited, so that his spoon continually clattered on the soup plate, impeding conversation. Already embarrassed, he reached down to pick up what he thought was the white napkin of his neighbour only to find it was the hem of her petticoat. In a sudden silence he could hear Virginia's voice clearly asking a guest: 'What do you mean by the Holy Ghost?' The angry response was 'I said "the whole coast".' The evening was a fiasco.

By the late 1920s, Virginia's income had increased considerably and she began to allocate income from sales to particular purchases. In September 1926 she gleefully reported that her American publisher was still selling large numbers of *Mrs Dalloway* and *The Common Reader*, four months after publication. It was the first year Virginia had earned more than Leonard. All of this could be translated into improvements at Monk's House. What those would be led to a critical change in their financial arrangements.

This was when Virginia recorded her irritation with Leonard's suggestion that increased income could pay for a full-time gardener and a cottage for him. Virginia, on the other hand, did not want to spend on gardens when there was still a lack of rugs, beds and good armchairs. It was an awkward and upsetting confrontation but Virginia remained resolute about the dispute, clear-eyed about the wider context of freedom and fairness: giving way on such a matter, as wives often did, she averred, could lead to grudges.

So that month Leonard devised a new system whereby, after apportioning expenses jointly (for rent, rates, doctors and clothes allowances, along with such necessities as new drains), they would at year-end calculate combined income and divide the excess into personal 'hoards'. Leonard, for example, would usually pay for garden expenses out of his; out of her hoard of £60 at the end of 1927, Virginia bought a bed from Heal's in Tottenham Court Road, as well as a cupboard, a strip of carpet for the hall of Tavistock Square, and a fur coat. She now had an impulse for making money for particular purposes: 'Leonard shall have his new car,' she wrote after a batch of good reviews. She had a chequebook – it was, she reflected, the first money of her own since she married, and she was enjoying her new spending power, allowing herself small treats. She liked buying stationery – but also furniture. One day she itemized her purchases – earrings (after getting her ears pierced with Vita), a brooch, a necklace, as well as carpeting for the dining room – and she derived great satisfaction from buying a rosewood and satinwood secretaire at a house sale. In mid-1929 she calculated her earnings, based on the previous six months, as being almost equivalent to that of a Cabinet Minister – but still thought the greatest pleasure of prosperity was being able to go and buy a pocketknife.

However, she still had anxieties, finding 'the money psychology' was odd. The 'spending muscle' after years of frugality, did not always work naturally. When, much later (in 1938), she made a large loan to a needy friend, her first instinct was to go out and buy herself a bookcase. But almost as quickly she bemoaned her generosity, calculating how many articles she must write to replenish her hoard, and continually fretting and regretting.

The agreement over finances with Leonard was not only a sign of her increasing independence, but an indication of their unique relationship. Her reliance on Leonard's care for her was paramount, but she also had a strong urge to forge her own way. One such impulse took her suddenly to Dieppe for three days to stay with artists Ethel Sands and Nan Hudson, describing the house with her usual interest – house painted in blues and greens, bright rugs, great pots of flowers carefully arranged by their butler. But she was always glad to get back to Leonard. In October 1937, she had an urge for a trip to Paris – but she changed her plan when she realized that Leonard didn't want her to go. She was 'overcome' with happiness as they walked round Tavistock Square, Virginia revelling in the realization that still after twenty-five years they couldn't bear to be separate: 'it's an enormous pleasure, being wanted: a wife.'

Nowhere are these competing needs – for care and independence – more strikingly shown than in her relationship with Vita Sackville-West. Vita had fallen for Virginia and, though a decade younger, felt protective of her, which accorded with Virginia's needs. The friendship had been growing fast since Vita became a Hogarth author. In December 1925, just after Vita's husband, Harold Nicolson, had left England to take up a diplomatic post in Tehran, Virginia went to stay with Vita at her home Long Barn, near Knole, bearing a note from Leonard: 'I enclose Virginia and I hope she behaves.' The only thing he asked was that Virginia be in bed by 11p.m. That didn't happen. Virginia and Vita talked until 3a.m., and it is probable that this is when their friendship developed into an affair, but Leonard remained sensibly forbearing. He joined them for the last day of the stay, and Vita drove the Woolfs back to London. Just as Harold also felt about Vita, Leonard was content with this relationship if it added to Virginia's happiness, while always alert for danger. However, Vita too was cautious, terrified of being the cause of a breakdown.

The only time Leonard appeared apprehensive was in 1928 when Virginia and Vita went for a week to Burgundy (where Virginia bought Leonard a green corduroy jacket) when, in fact, the affair had run its course. Virginia's affection for Leonard was undimmed. Even after a tryst with Vita she was 'all of a quiver' at coming home to Leonard, and amazed at her happiness: 'I have had a good draught of human life, & find much champagne in it. It has not been dull – my marriage; not at all.'

Early in their friendship, Vita had taken Virginia to stay at Knole, the extraordinary mansion that held such sway over Vita. Its time-linked architecture (365 bedrooms, 52 staircases, seven courtyards) was stunning, though Virginia had reservations about the smallish rooms, feeling that they had not enough beauty. But the elaborate decoration, fabulous furnishings and ancient tapestries, as well as the long gallery, the silver bedroom (though Vita found that a little 'vulgar') and, above all, its connections with monarchs of the past nevertheless had an impact, and the remarkable result was *Orlando*. The plot came to Virginia the following year on the last day of their summer in Monk's House, 5 October 1927, and contributed to what Virginia called the '*happiest* autumn'. It began as a joke, she said, but almost immediately she plunged into plotting a fantastical biography starting in 1500, spanning three centuries and with a sex change of her hero (a missive for our times). Vita, as narcissistic as she was generous, gave her wholehearted endorsement to the book, which brought life to Knole, vividly detailing its rich interior (for example 'the gallery whose floor was laid with whole oak trees sawn across', as Vita believed), and gave Vita an unmatchable gift of somehow making the house her own, just as it was lost to her forever: while the book was being written, Vita's father died, in January 1928, and Knole passed to his brother and out of Vita's world.

For Virginia, the chance to write about Knole and its importance in Vita's life was a way of encapsulating the attitude and many of the themes shared by Virginia and Leonard on the importance of houses. It was when she was in the heady throes of writing *Orlando* that she had come to the realization that she was rationally thinking that she did not regret not having children – more important to her was to write without interruption: 'My ideas so possess me.' The process of writing was a chance of spending time with Vita, researching and checking, but also a way of relinquishing her passion for her too. Just as in *To the Lighthouse*, when she had

Virginia with Vita Sackville-West, Hogarth Press author and close friend, at Monk's House.

The first cover of *Orlando* was, unusually, not designed by Vanessa but was in keeping with its billing as 'a biography'.

laid the ghosts of her father and mother, so it seems to have been with *Orlando*. Having turned this experience into copy – and highly remunerative copy – the bodily passions cooled. Vita had already romped on to other lovers in her casually carnal way, though their mutual affection endured. The two couples remained friendly: they made a joint expedition by special train to Yorkshire in June 1927 to see the total eclipse. Leonard and Virginia visited Berlin when Harold was at the embassy there.

Published in 1928 to great acclaim, *Orlando* sold 8,000 copies in the first six months. By December there were plans for a third edition. *Orlando* delighted Vita: 'I am in love with Orlando – this is a complication I had not foreseen . . . you made me cry with your passages about Knole.'

Virginia mused on the change in the relationship. The excitement had gone, yet the relationship was 'saner, perhaps deeper'. However, by 1935, she felt that her passionate friendship was over, curiously, in a way, perhaps because Vita became preoccupied with Sissinghurst Castle, her new home, a sixteenth-century ruin in Kent that had no running water and barely a single room habitable, rather like Monk's House when Virginia and Leonard moved in. In 1932 they both visited Sissinghurst for lunch to see the progress. Though Virginia admired Vita's tower (which contained her workroom) with its 'lovely pink brick', she did not have the same covetous reaction as she sometimes had when visiting friends' houses: like Knole – and unlike Monk's House – it had no view.

The enjoyable surge of writing *Orlando* was very unlike the process of writing *The Waves*, which had started out with the working title of *The Moths*, because

Vita and Virginia, with Vita's sons Benedict (left) and Nigel, at Vita's new home of Sissinghurst Castle.

Writing *The Waves* was agonising – but it was a great success on publication.

the seeds had been sown by a letter that Vanessa had written from Cassis, where she now had a summer home, about a moth flying into a candle, which prompted memories of the Stephen children's moth-hunting expeditions. She teased the ideas out over several years, producing her most experimental work, a series of soliloquies by six characters from childhood onwards, interspersed by interludes describing sun and sea from dawn to dusk. The characters were modelled, as was often the case, on close associates: Susan is very like Vanessa, Neville has aspects of Lytton. There is a seventh character, silent but referred to by the others: Percival, who dies halfway through the novel and is based on her brother Thoby (already memorialized in *Jacob's Room*). She found it totally draining. As she had done before, she leavened the fiction with factual writing: in October 1927, she had presented two papers on women and fiction at Cambridge University – which two years later were published as *A Room of One's Own*, one of Virginia's most influential books. It outdid *Orlando*.

She returned to *The Waves*. And in January 1931, 'on this first day of being 49', she had suddenly seen the 'entire book whole', realizing how she could finish it in three weeks and how her mind would 'again be free' and she would be able to 'read again with all my mind'. In fact it was finished sooner, on 7 February – though there was, of course, the inevitable rewriting, the disappointment over its low calibre, the conviction that it would be badly received, before giving it to Leonard to read. On 19 July, Leonard came into her garden workroom at Monk's House full of praise. Published on 8 October, it sold 5,000 in the first week and was already reprinting. She remained uncertain. How odd, she thought, after noting the good *Times* review, that people can read 'that difficult grinding stuff'. But Forster wrote a letter that thrilled her: 'I've the sort of excitement over it which comes from believing that one's encountered a classic.'

1932 was the year her reputation was secured. It began well: she felt prolific with '5 books in my mind', likening herself to Dickens. Books about her work were published in English (by Winifred Holtby, who had worked at the Press), German and French. She was asked by Trinity College to deliver the Ford Clark lectures: this was a particular accolade as her father had given the first series in 1883. 'Think of me, the uneducated child reading books in my room at 22 H.P.G. – now advanced to this glory.' She refused, though dithered over her decision later. As a matter of course, she declined honours and prestigious positions, such as chairing PEN, the writers' association.

As respite from revising and correcting *The Waves*, she had begun *Flush*, a fictional biography of Elizabeth Barrett Browning's spaniel from the dog's point of view, extensively based on the author's letters. It was destined to pay for repairs to the pond and for paving of the front garden at Monk's House. She continued to work on it as light relief from the early emergence of her next book, already brewing, already agonising – *The Years*. *Flush* was published in 1933, with Pinka modelling for pictures. Inevitably, she was dissatisfied with the final version, so she was much cheered by David Garnett's comment on her 'delightful humour' – and days later kept awake by *Granta*'s verdict that it represented 'the end of Mrs Woolf as a live force'. She was always sensitive to criticism, always seesawing from pleasure to depression. However, *Flush* sold well – and also paid for the Italian garden, inspired by a trip to Tuscany that year.

*The Years*, first referred to as *The Pargiters* and becoming briefly *Other People's Houses*, with its echoes of Kensington, 22 Hyde Park Gate and the household there, proved to be an almost insuperable ordeal. It took four years. At her best, she was simply frustrated and longed to be rid of it, to get on to her next project: she was incubating a wish to write an anti-fascist pamphlet, and then her ideas coalesced after a chance meeting with Forster at the London Library in April 1935. He told her that ladies would not be allowed on the committee as the committee had agreed that 'ladies are quite impossible'. Infuriated, she was spurred into developing an essay on 'Being Despised' and thence into a consideration of a Society of Outsiders and pacifism in her anti-war and pro-women polemic *Three Guineas*. Leonard described it as 'impeccable feminism'.

At her worst in the final stages of *The Years* she came as near to madness, as near to suicide she herself said, as she was after the publication of her first book, comparing her 'acute despair' to that she had on rereading her first book *The Voyage Out*: Leonard said it was a terrifying time. The rewriting was draining: 'I think I've finished it, and then it springs back in my face, like a bramble, all prickles, and I have to begin again, cutting and pruning.' Discovering that she had not made enough to pay her share of the house and so had to dip into her hoard, was not helpful. So it was an immense relief that Leonard called it 'a most remarkable book' – though he said in his autobiography that his opinion was that it was not as good as her other novels. But she needed that constant reassurance to continue; in fact, a week after it was published on 11 March 1937, it was being hailed as a masterpiece; it sold 25,000 in two months and a month later it was the bestselling book in America.

To add to her jangled state at the start of writing *The Years*, Bedford Estates was insisting on improvements to the house, including decoration and a new electric boiler. All books had to be moved, carpets rolled up, with workmen everywhere. What was worse was the visit from the surveyor who said the weight of their books would require ceilings to be shored up with an iron pillar. There were months when they felt as though they were camping. All meals, which they had to eat on their knees, seemed to taste of plaster: Nellie was decidedly not pleased. That was the year, 1934, that Nellie was finally dismissed, after a row about an electric oven that the Woolfs wanted to try – but she didn't. It ended the tumultuous relationship, but it was not, of course, the end of servants. Mabel Haskins came, recommended by Margery Fry, and stayed for six years – though she was scared of Leonard. Curiously Leonard, despite his lifelong work for the Labour Party and equality, was quite hard on the servants, which was a puzzle to Virginia. Virginia was the peacemaker, the arbitrator, pouring oil on troubled waters, though when Mabel trod on Leonard's spectacles she had to go . . .

Virginia with composer and close friend Dame Ethel Smyth at Monk's House.

1934 was a year when she felt inundated. Recognition is what she had craved, but she felt the drag of fame. Fame 'means nothing' and yet took up too much time. The letters she longed for increasingly contained requests, demands and invitations. She found them hard to resist. One letter in February 1934 was from Cyril Connolly who was giving a cocktail party to meet their lemurs. That is one invitation she did turn down.

Virginia had visitors almost every day, including the composer Dame Ethel Smyth, twenty-four years older and deaf, who barged into her life after self-confessedly falling in love with Virginia after reading *A Room of One's Own*; Virginia, in turn, respected Ethel's fight for women's rights. Ethel was very forthright but also perceptive – which led her to tell Virginia bluntly that she focused too much on herself. She was to become a close friend and constant correspondent but continually hounded her for meetings in between telling Virginia that she must learn to curtail social engagements to protect herself. Virginia wrote about one projected meeting: 'think of me talking at the top of my voice and listening at the top of my ears for the next 6 hours.' Leonard was irritated by her, and so, often, was Virginia. The sojourns in Monk's House provided some respite from her, and from the social whirl in general, though it was perhaps not far enough.

What did provide relief were the holidays every year to Italy, Greece (including the thrill of a visit to Delphi), Spain or France: Montaigne's tower, with its three-windowed library and wonderful view at Brantôme proved a powerful experience for Virginia, who had long admired him. They drove round Scotland – she finally did visit Skye, where she wryly acknowledged its difference from Cornwall – and Ireland, where they visited Elizabeth Bowen (and considered buying a house in Glengarriff). There were several visits to Cassis, where Vanessa had set up an outpost of Charleston. On one trip, Virginia planned to buy La Boudarde, a whitewashed villa near Fontcreuse, fantasizing about Leonard in shirtsleeves, and watching the sardine boats come in. But she was glad to return to the English spring: 'garden blazing with lilac, apple, pear blossom, and every flower you can imagine,' as she wrote to Vanessa on her return home.

There were constant family events. She accompanied Leonard sometimes on his conscientious fortnightly trips to Worthing to visit his mother 'as spry as a weasel', even in old age. They visited Waddesdon, home of the Rothschild family, where Leonard's brother Philip was land agent; Cecil, Philip's son, remembers as a child taking Virginia to the grotto where they tested echoes by calling Ce-cil, Vir-ginia. She often walked to Charleston to see Vanessa, or they would meet in a Bloomsbury square: Vanessa had rooms in Gordon Square and a studio in Fitzroy Square. Vanessa's studio was the venue for the one and only performance of *Freshwater*, resurrected and rewritten for Angelica's seventeenth birthday party in 1935. It was a comedy based on the Freshwater Circle of artists and poets on the Isle of Wight, featuring her great-aunt Julia Margaret Cameron (Vanessa), Tennyson (Adrian) and Ellen Terry: Angelica played Ellen Terry and Julian (about to depart for China for a post teaching English at Wuhan University) the handsome young naval lieutenant she decides to run away with. Virginia prompted.

In 1936 they drove to Germany, an admittedly risky adventure – particularly because, as Virginia wrote, 'people say we might be unpopular as we are Jews' – where they saw for themselves the ubiquity of the Nazi influence, and anti-semitic posters in every town. They had taken the precaution of taking diplomatic letters with them in case of difficulty, but any unwelcome attention was deflected by the recent addition to the household – Mitz the marmoset, who clung to Leonard's neck as he drove, causing curiosity and mirth – and, often, averting the need for papers.

Leonard, always fond of animals, had made the acquaintance of Mitz two years earlier at a lunch with friends, who then asked Leonard to look after him in their absence on holiday. Leonard, who felt the marmoset was 'rather rickety', nursed him back to health and then refused to return him. Mitz was devoted to Leonard, though not to Virginia:

Mitz the marmoset, so beloved by Leonard, peering out of the window in Italy.

once when Mitz was up a tree as they were about to leave Rodmell, Leonard coaxed him down by kissing Virginia: 'Mitz came down as fast as she could and jumped on my shoulder.' Virginia had mixed feelings, often finding herself on errands to Gamages' department store in Holborn to buy worms for Mitz. On their return to Monk's House after their German trip with Mitz, they found Pinka had died the day before, causing great sadness, particularly for Leonard. Weeks later they bought another cocker spaniel, Sally, who was at once passionately attached to Leonard.

The 1930s had brought much personal grief: shatteringly the death in 1932 of Lytton Strachey, so close once to both Virginia and Leonard, and then, in 1934, of Roger Fry, after which Virginia was prevailed upon by Roger's sister, Margery, to write his biography. At first unwilling, she agreed and was assiduous in her efforts. And in her usual manner of balancing fact and fiction, she began to toy with a new novel, calling it *Pointz Hall*. The biography took several years to complete, but – despite Leonard's unusual disapproval of the book (Virginia said he had been very severe) – it became immediately successful on its publication in 1940.

Most traumatic of all, however, had been the shocking death in 1937 of Julian Bell, who had enlisted in June as an ambulance driver in the Spanish Civil War, and was killed by shrapnel a month later. For Virginia, the future without Julian was 'cut off, lopped'. Vanessa collapsed utterly and it was Virginia who looked after her sister through the next months, just as Vanessa had once looked after her. It was a significant shift in the chequered relationship, and one that Vanessa valued – though curiously she did not say this to Virginia directly, but through Vita. Duncan also wrote to her to thank her for her letters at this time, which 'have been the salt of our life'.

The background to the 1930s for the Woolfs was more house-hunting. Forewarned in 1930 that there were plans to demolish the south side of Tavistock Square to make way for offices, they searched intermittently for another home for themselves and the Press, looking over premises in Russell Square and Gordon Square. One was at 47 Gordon Square, next door to Virginia's first Bloomsbury home, but their offer was turned down by Bedford Estates because of their publishing business: it would, in their view, bring too many vans into a more secluded square. Later they looked at another on the corner of Gordon Square with a warren of a basement and an entrance on another street so that objection did not apply.

Demolition of 52 was deferred, but in September 1938 they were given notice to quit. Virginia and Leonard found a pleasant and quiet house with, Leonard thought, a particularly beautiful outlook in Mecklenburgh Square, the eastern twin of Brunswick Square. After installing wiring and a kitchen, as well as planning a new bathroom, they moved to 37 Mecklenburgh Square in May 1939, accompanied by the solicitors Dollman and Pritchard. In September 1940 it was heavily damaged by a bomb dropped on the next-door house. Hogarth Press was installed at their printers in Letchworth, and Virginia and Leonard moved completely to Monk's House.

This portrait of Leonard at work with his spaniel, Sally, at his side was painted by Vanessa in 1940.

# A House of One's Own – Monk's House

*'There's nothing I enjoy more than looking for houses'*

---

As soon as Monk's House had become theirs in 1919, Virginia wrote to Ka Cox under the letter heading: 'That will be our address for ever and ever; indeed I've already marked out our graves.' Their mood was buoyant. Quite soon after arrival, they named the two elm trees by the boundary, their branches intertwined, Virginia and Leonard.

On the day they moved in, 1 September 1919, Vanessa had suggested that Virginia come over to Charleston. But Virginia had refused to be dislodged: 'Leonard quite agrees with you that I shall be merely in the way during the move. I, on the other hand, think myself indispensable.'

The move was accomplished with the help of farm bailiff Frank Gunn and his farm cart. It took two wagonloads to transport the household across the Southease Bridge from Asheham to Rodmell and into Monk's House. They had already acquired some items at the house sale of its contents in August: Leonard's interests were mostly on the garden side (he bid for tools, baskets and apple trays) but there were also purchases of an oil stove, table and twelve bone-handled knives and six forks for nineteen shillings. They bought, for four shillings, three paintings that had originally belonged to the Glazebrook family, who had lived there from 1796–1877, including one of the family, so coveted by their friend Morgan Forster that it was lent to him and hung on the wall of his rooms at King's College, Cambridge, for many years. The other two pictures, of a man holding his horse by its reins, and

Monk's House, purchased in 1919, was to be Virginia's home for the rest of her life.

The two elm trees on the edge of their land had intertwined branches and therefore were named Leonard and Virginia.

a lady, are echoed in *Between the Acts,* Virginia's last novel. All of these paintings can still be seen at Monk's House.

Leonard from the start was very taken with their new home; he had the same feeling for it as for Hogarth House about the continuity of people living there: 'one became part of history and of a civilisation by continuing in the line of all their lives.' The people who had built and lived in the house had left 'the aura of their lives, imposing their personality on the rooms, as though it were a work of art.' He found both houses peaceful – and was certain that the calm that permeated the house and garden helped stabilize Virginia's mind and health. 'I am sure that this tranquil atmosphere helped to tranquilize her mind.'

They had hopes of the name – Virginia was convinced that the niches by the fireplace in the main room were for holy water. The twelfth-century St Peter's Church, at the end of their garden, once belonged to the Cluniac Priory of St

In 1934 Virginia's writing lodge was built at the end of the garden by the wall of St Peter's Church.

Pancras at Lewes, so it was feasible that the property might have been used as a retreat for the monks of Lewes Priory, but Leonard dismissed this as he could find no indication in the deeds. It was also suggested, perhaps more plausibly, that its original incarnation was as three agricultural workers' cottages. This was credible as it was a house of many doors and many levels (seven, one subsequent resident calculated). Small rooms led into each other, down or up steps, through low doorways. The house also had the feeling of being integrated with its land, as flower beds were close to the windows of the sitting room, which was set below the level of the garden: Angelica thought 'one stepped into it rather as one steps into a boat'.

There were many problems to solve in the long-neglected house where they were to live during the summer months. There was no bath and the earth closet was some distance from the house through 'a winding glade'. The last owner had done his own repairs – when he had done any. Jacob Verrall, stalwart of the parish, had lived alone for years until his death at the age of seventy-four. Leonard likened him to the sort of unknown rustic villager described in Gray's *Elegy in a Country Churchyard,* and was taken by the story that he had spent the last months of his life lying in bed with a bell attached to his toe to frighten away birds if they landed on his cherry tree, which he could see through his bedroom window.

Work began with removing some of the thin partitions between the rooms to create a large sitting room. But the first real problem was the kitchen. It had five brick steps up to the garden, down which rain would cascade, finding its way across the room and leaking out into the street. One of the first tasks for Virginia, while Leonard was away on Hogarth Press business, was to supervise Christopher Dean, the local builder and blacksmith, in his efforts to cure that. He also installed a new sink. There was a kitchen range but no stove. For several weeks their meals (mainly stews) were provided by the sexton's wife, Mrs Dedman (mother of 11 children), who brought them over piping hot. Over the following years, when Nellie did not accompany them, they relied a great deal on the services of local women, such as Rose Bartholomew, whose brother Percy became Leonard's full-time gardener in 1928 (William Dedman had helped out to begin with). Ham and eggs seem to have been on the menu quite a lot. Along with an 'odious' pudding called Canary (a traditional steamed pudding).

In October the Woolfs returned to Hogarth House for the winter to be told that the lease of the house was to be terminated. As it turned out, by the end of 1919 they had bought both Hogarth House and its neighbour Suffield House. Virginia rather revelled in this frenzy of property acquisition, casually adding at the end of a letter to Lytton that 'we've got to buy 2 more houses'. She had earlier written to Janet Case: 'Did Leonard tell you how we bought a house in Lewes, and then saw one we liked better at Rodmell, and so bought that, and have now sold the first house, and have only 3 cottages in Cornwall, and Asheham, and the house in Rodmell and Hogarth House to live in?'

Since Virginia was still part-owner of 22 Hyde Park Gate (sold in 1928 for £4,925), it was a feat to almost rival Agatha Christie, who at one time owned eight houses – but she was a great deal wealthier than the Woolfs, who at this point were

Steps from the kitchen at Monk's House led up to the garden – and, in later years, to Virginia's bedroom round the corner.

on an income of about £700 a year. The Cornish cottages had to go. There is no indication that they ever visited the cottages before they were sold.

Conditions at Monk's House were primitive. The earth closet in the garden was replaced in 1922 by one closer to the house. They set up another one in the loft by placing a cane chair over a bucket. A tin tub behind a curtain in the kitchen was where they bathed. Lighting was by Aladdin oil lamps. Mice were a problem, keeping them awake at night. Leonard and Virginia, who at Asheham had shared a bed, were at first sharing a room in separate beds (later, when Lottie had left their employ, Leonard moved into another room). As Leonard made his bed one night, a mouse jumped out from among the blankets.

In 1930 when a two-storey extension was added to the house, this was intended as her writing room but a year later became her bedroom.

Virginia's favourite project was painting, just as with other houses. First the stairs: white, with blue banisters; then the dining room, distempered the colour of pomegranates. At one point, she tells Vanessa, perhaps provocatively, that she is going to paint the house bright yellow – though this seems to have been confined to yellow-washing the earth closet one summer afternoon.

It was a remarkably sunny house compared to Asheham, which had been sheltered deep in beech woods at the bottom of a coombe, while Monk's House had huge views over to the Downs across the Brooks, so called because of the drainage channels and creeks that took the overflow from the Ouse at high tide. Fond though Virginia had been of Asheham, she admitted to the delight of having the sun flooding into the house and the sound of village cricket matches. She now noticed how the dampness of the air at Asheham had affected their books. She was loving the 'bells ringing for church – daffodils out – apple trees in blossom – cows mooing – cocks crowing – thrushes chirping' – though she became impatient with the 'jangling' bells.

The first major improvement at Monk's House was in the summer of 1920 when the kitchen was overhauled and a solid fuel stove installed. (This went some way to make it more acceptable to Nellie, who found Monk's House even more inconvenient than Asheham.) As her earning power increased, Virginia was linking that to alterations – just as Agatha Christie was doing at about the same time. In her autobiography, Agatha wrote: 'The nice part about writing in those days [the 1920s] was that I directly related it to money. This stimulated my output enormously.' She would, for example, decide that she'd like a loggia. She'd get an estimate, then plan a story. 'In due course I wrote it, and then I had my loggia.'

The spur for Virginia's creativity was not so directly financial, but in 1925 she wrote in her diary: 'I'm out to make £300 this summer by writing, & build a bath & hot water range at Rodmell.' Thanks to the sales of *Mrs Dalloway* and *The Common Reader*, Philcox Bros of Lewes, founded the year they moved in (and still trading), was commissioned the following spring to install a hot water boiler and tank, and to squeeze into the little room over the kitchen a bath with curly feet, a sink and a toilet, as well as upgrading the outside lavatory with a flush, plus new drains and cesspool. By April 1926, she was contemplating with jubilation the end of seven years of having to go outside to the toilet and planning a grand opening party when the toilets would be flushed and the hot water would flow for the first time.

In fact, of course, there was a last-minute drama as the well fell in and Leonard had to rush down to Rodmell to deal with it. (Monk's House was finally connected to the water mains in 1934.) But by the end of May, they were luxuriating in hot water 'in torrents, boiling hot, for every conceivable purpose'. Even Nellie was satisfied. In the morning after breakfast Virginia would bath, using the time to talk through scenes she had thought of in the night. Vita visited them that June

and wrote to Harold of Leonard and Virginia's glee: 'They both run upstairs every now and then and pull the plug just for the sheer fun of it and come down and say "It worked very well that time – did you hear?"'

In addition, alterations were made to the drawing room, knocking two rooms into one, to make a sitting/dining room. (Different bricks on the floor show where the division was.) Virginia sought advice from Vanessa on the new room, asking

At one side of the large sitting room was Leonard's desk, and by the fireplace he and Virginia each had their favourite chair. Much of the furniture was commissioned from Vanessa Bell and Duncan Grant.

deferentially what curtains to get, what chair covers. 'Would I be allowed some rather garish but vibrating and radiating green and red lustres on the mantelpiece? Showers of glass, shaped like long fingers in a bunch – you know my taste that way.' She also wanted to buy a ship in a glass bottle and a mother of pearl and wooden platter: 'But I will wait for you.'

She painted the room sea-green, a colour she was always fond of, which gave it an underwater air. The final effect delighted her, approving of the beams (also green) down the middle, the five windows, and 'flowers & leaves nodding in all around us'. She wrote with satisfaction: 'at last I like looking at the drawing room. I like my rug; my carpet; my painted beams.'

Virginia relied a great deal on Vanessa's expertise. Quite early, she asked her sister to design a cushion for her, enclosing a rough sketch and the measurements: she wanted something to work on while staying in Rodmell. Virginia enjoyed needlework, worked on tapestries, and once made a patchwork quilt, and also took up knitting. Perhaps the cushion design was the one described by Vita in a letter to her husband Harold written while she stayed in Rodmell in June 1926: 'She is sitting opposite me embroidering a rose, a black lace fan, a box of matches, and four playing cards, on a mauve canvas background, from a design by her sister.' Virginia commissioned furniture and pottery from Vanessa and Duncan (though she sometimes had to pursue Vanessa to bill her properly) – a painted dining table, a tiled low table and chairs, many of which are still at Monk's House. The backs of the dining chairs have a design of a bowl of flowers by Vanessa and were embroidered by Duncan's mother, Ethel Grant.

Virginia was right about Leonard – his efforts were focused on the garden. Greenhouses went up. Outhouses came down – except for one tool shed by the edge of the garden. According to Marie Bartholomew, daughter of Percy Bartholomew the gardener, the roof had to be replaced, which gave Leonard the chance to install an apple loft, accessed by a wooden staircase at the side. The shed itself became a writing room for Virginia, with a window carved out to frame

The small ground-floor guest bedroom was turned into the dining room in 1926. The backs of the chairs were designed by Vanessa and embroidered by Duncan Grant's mother, Ethel.

The French doors of the writing lodge opened onto a terrace, often used by guests. (Left to right) Angelica, Vanessa, Clive and Virginia.

the view across the valley. It was fairly Spartan: even in August an oil stove was necessary to combat the chill – and Leonard's autumn ritual of laying out the apples caused irritation to Virginia as she was disturbed.

Some half-walls of flint from the outhouses, such as the one from the piggery, still with its small square entrance, were retained and the effect, along with hedging, was of a series of garden rooms, reminiscent, perhaps, of the Talland House garden. Leonard was never happier than when he was in his garden. He even took up topiary, patiently clipping the yew hedge into the shape of a recumbent peacock. The orchard, as they had anticipated, was bountiful, yielding plums, pears, cherries, apples and figs – and starred in her short story 'In the Orchard', alluding to the children reciting their tables from the school across the wall and the 'sharp squeak' of the church weathervane. Later, a fishpond was added; it was Leonard's pride – in 1929 there were four goldfish and one carp – but also Virginia's joy; her short story 'The Fascination of the Pool', was written in the same year. Statues were bought, many from Ballard's general store in Barcombe, near Lewes, and dotted about the garden.

Virginia scheduled twice-weekly walks to entice Leonard from the garden, but also joined in the work, testifying to the joy of weeding on spring evenings: 'we

Leonard left walls from the dismantled outhouses to make a series of garden 'rooms'.

giggle and joke, and go and poke at roots and plan beds of nasturtiums.' She talked of the pleasure of earth under her nails, and 'weeding all day to finish the beds in a queer sort of enthusiasm which made me say this is happiness.' The scratches and stiffness the day after one marathon stint were a badge of honour.

There were, however, recurring skirmishes over greenhouses. It was Leonard's desire for one, as well as a full-time gardener, that had led to the argument that resulted in the rearrangement of their finances, and consequently to Virginia's sense of financial freedom. Leonard's hoard paid for the gardener, Percy Bartholomew, appointed in 1928, and living in one of the pair of houses – 1 and 2 Park Cottages – bought in 1926.

For Virginia, the pleasure was in buying items of furniture. 'For years I never had a pound extra; a comfortable bed, or a chair that did not want stuffing.' But on Tuesday, 2 September 1930 Hammonds in Lewes delivered four armchairs. It must have been a deeply satisfying moment. There was also the purchase of Heal's chairs (one in beech with curved arms is now in the sitting room at Monk's House). There was great excitement at the unexpected arrival of a desk sent by Ethel Sands who had heard that Virginia had been let down over a desk that she had commissioned. When the crate was delivered from Paris by way of Newhaven, both Leonard and Virginia went running off to find a hammer each to attack the packing case. It was a desk that she waxed lyrical over, one with fourteen drawers and a lid. It even fitted exactly by her window. 'Your desk is the joy of my life,' she wrote to Ethel.

In 1926 she bought an inflatable boat for jaunts on the River Ouse. Six years later, they bought a rather more expensive rubber dinghy (she was rather shocked at the price, £7 7s 6d) and she and Julian took it out the day after it arrived. There were very happy times at Monk's House, though times of extreme anxiety too – for both of them. Once, Virginia fainted in the garden and she noted, as she came round, Leonard looking 'very frightened'. Put to bed, she had a 'season of silence' and comforted herself with the thought that 'brooding is a form of fertilisation.' There was also concern about Leonard's health when it appeared he had kidney disease. He was unwell for some months, but after visits to specialists was given the all-clear.

Monk's House was, at first, mainly a summer home, though they did visit at Easter, and sometimes at Christmas. They usually travelled down by train to Lewes and then on the small branch line to Seaford, alighting at the halt at Southease, a mile or so from Rodmell (though they sometimes had trouble because of crowded trains). In the summer, the journey might be by 'reserved saloon': Virginia wrote to a friend in the summer of 1923, that they were 'All packed to go to Sussex tomorrow. We travel with a selection of our books packed in hampers. Add to this a dog and a tortoise, bought for 2/- yesterday in the High Street.' But circumstances changed: in July 1927, on the strength of sales of *To the Lighthouse* (advance sales were 1,690, twice that of *Mrs Dalloway*; by July sales were 4,000) they bought a car.

Acquiring a car had been under discussion for a couple of years. Virginia thought it would boost her independence, and anyway Vanessa was already driving a Renault. Virginia and Leonard began driving lessons at the same time. Virginia, who reported that her gear changing was very good, was 'wobbling round and round Windmill Hill every day' and seemed confident enough that by July, she was feeling that she had learnt enough to drive a car in the country alone. But only Leonard was the eventual driver.

Their first car was a dark blue Singer, nicknamed Lighthouse, or Umbrella. According to one of Vita's letters, Leonard toyed with the idea of garaging it in Virginia's studio at Tavistock Square, an idea that received short shrift. Two years later it was replaced by a new Singer with a sunshine roof, and in 1933 by a Lanchester – green and silver and sleek: 'It glides with the smoothness of an eel, with the speed of a swift and the – isn't this a good blurb? – the power of a tigress,' she wrote to Vita.

Their habits changed. The afternoon walks were replaced by afternoon drives. The car would be greased and cleaned before their runs round the countryside, and for some time, Virginia noted, the conversation was all of gears and cylinders, petrol and picnics. The pleasures were legion: sandwiches by the roadside; lunch in the Mermaid Inn in Rye; the bliss of sitting in the front seat with the windscreen open. She wrote of the pleasures in 'Evening Over Sussex: Reflections in a Motor Car' in 1930, though it was not published until after her death.

Their third car, bought in 1933, was a Lanchester, driven only by Leonard though Virginia had learned to drive in their first car.

Virginia loved the glimpses, passing though they may be, into other lives in villages or past fine houses like the eighteenth-century Groombridge Place as they made enthusiastic expeditions all over Sussex, Kent and the south of England. It was, she said, 'the joy of our lives, an additional life, free & mobile & airy to live alongside our usual stationary industry. We spin off to Falmer, ride over the downs, drop into Rottingdean, sweep over to Seaford, call, in pouring rain, at Charleston . . . return for tea, all as light & easy as a hawk in the air.'

She may not have had the independence of driving a car herself, but she did get a room of her own. Virginia had promised herself this if she made money from *Orlando* – and she did: it outsold all her previous books, and she could pay for it. The architect George Kennedy (uncle of Richard Kennedy, who was just then working at the Hogarth Press) stayed with them at Rodmell for a night after Christmas 1928 to discuss adding a workroom for her. They spent two hours in the attics planning the addition, which, in the end, became a two-storey extension at the side of the house, with bedroom for her above. They approached a local builder in Lewes in March; in April Virginia was writing to Vanessa that 'Philcox came out and drew a sketch of two rooms in a jiffy', and planned to have completion by August.

Leonard had improvised a study for himself over what was the coach-house and now the garage, according to Vita, by merging three small rooms into one: it met with approval by Vita when he invited her to see the result on her visit to Monk's House in August 1929. Virginia, meanwhile, was full of excitement over doors, windows, cupboards and handles for her room. Regular updates were provided by Percy. On their visit in early December the roof was on, floors made and the windows in. Tiles from Vanessa, a birthday present, adorned the two fireplaces: a lighthouse and a ship for the downstairs room and fruit and flowers for the bedroom.

Shortly after the publication of *A Room of One's Own* in October 1929 (it sold 22,000 copies in the first six months), Virginia had two rooms of her own: on Boxing Day in 1929 she was luxuriating in her new bedroom, with fire, table and new curtains at the windows framing two enormous views over the water meadows and towards the church. But by the end of the following summer, Virginia had

Virginia reading, in the extension's upstairs room, by the fireplace with its tiles painted by Vanessa for Virginia's birthday.

decided to swap the rooms round so that her bedroom became a sitting room: to waste the view during the day seemed a crime. The upstairs sitting room under its sloping ceilings and full of light became a favourite spot for both Virginia and Leonard and their guests: John Lehmann described the shelves filled with books that Virginia had rebound in bright paper covers (a favourite pastime – and, as she admitted, 'occupational therapy'), tables piled with newspapers, books and Leonard's pot plants – begonias and lilies with their heady perfume – while

The new upstairs room was intended as Virginia's bedroom, but she decided the view was too good to keep to herself and so it became a sitting room.

Leonard puffed at his pipe and Virginia smoked her home-rolled cigarettes in a long holder.

The bedroom beneath was rather less convenient, though a washbasin with cupboard below was added. As there was no entrance from the house, she would climb the steps from the kitchen to the garden and turn left along the path to get to her bedroom. With its windows on two walls and door opening to the views of the church past the orchard, it felt to her as though she was in the garden. How happy she was after people went and she and Leonard sat alone, after which 'I would go to bed in my airy room, where the rising sun on the apples & asparagus wakes me, if I leave the curtain open.' Leonard would take her breakfast in the morning (in a mackintosh if it was raining) and they would talk about the day to come. Cecil, Leonard's nephew, remembers taking her breakfast and seeing scraps of paper everywhere, notes that she'd jotted down in the night.

1930 was a watershed year as far as Monk's House was concerned. For Virginia it was, she averred, 'the best, the freeest, the comfortablest summer we've ever had'. The main reason for her ease was Nellie's long absence due to convalescence after an operation: a young mother, Annie Thomsett, was cooking and cleaning for them instead and living in one of the Woolf's cottages. She was out of the house by 3p.m. – bliss for Virginia, who appreciated the additional novelty of their sleeping in an empty house. (Later, after Annie left, Louie Everest was employed as a housekeeper, living in that same cottage.)

In one of her many ruminations on the business of sharing life with servants, Virginia displayed some sympathy: 'It strikes me that one is absurd to expect good temper or magnanimity from servants, considering what crowded small rooms they live in, with their work all about them.' However, she was dreading Nellie's return: 'I think with real shrinking of having her in control again.' Virginia did not achieve the ideal that she hoped for – housework done without having to deal with servants – until later. But that summer of 1930 gave her the first indication that it might be possible.

Louie Everest (later Mayer) became the housekeeper in 1934 and stayed until Leonard's death in 1969.

What really made a difference to the household was the installation of the new kitchen stove, which she described in some wonder: 'At this moment it is cooking my dinner in the glass dishes perfectly I hope, without smell, waste, or confusion; one turns handles, there is a thermometer.' She actually broke off from her diary at one point to go and watch it cooking the ham. The simplicity of the new stove made her envisage a future free of cooks, more independence.

She would be able to 'come down here with a chop in a bag and live on my own.' She had a sudden enthusiasm for cooking, listing the dishes she would make – macaroni cheese, stews, sauces, and adventurous dishes with a dash of wine in them. Though she ate sparingly, her enthusiasm underlined her interest in food, shown in the mouthwatering description of *boeuf en daube* in *To the Lighthouse*. Hot rolls for breakfast made her 'the happiest woman in England'. She hunted for mushrooms, bottled fruit and potted honey. Cooking rather than book writing seemed so much more appealing. 'I make bread. I cook mushrooms. I wander in & out of the kitchen. I have a resource besides reading.'

What also helped the smooth running of the household was the installation of electricity in 1931, which meant no more oil lamps, but proper lighting (which Virginia had been used to in Gordon Square in 1905), electric fires in the bedrooms and, in 1935, an electric stove for the kitchen. In celebration she distempered the kitchen bright green ('rather a good colour') and a new window was added, overlooking the garden. Why had she never thought of doing that before, she wondered.

Other improvements included a refrigerator, a telephone and loudspeakers for the radiogram. In the evenings they would sit round the fire, and she would do her needlework while listening to classical music. She wrote to Vita about the happiness of Monk's House. 'I must go and put my pie in the oven; then we have ice-cream to follow – you know we have a Frigidaire – with fresh raspberries. Then we turn on the loudspeaker – Bach tonight – then I watch my baby owls learning to fly on the church tower.'

In October 1934, her old garden writing room was demolished by another local builder, Wicks and Sons of Lewes, and rebuilt as a lodge close to the churchyard wall, by a towering sweet chestnut tree. Glass doors led on to a small terrace, and a view over the marshes to Mount Caburn, the isolated hill that was one of the highest landmarks in Sussex. So taken with it was she that she even planned to sleep there on summer nights.

Mr Wicks was back, in 1938, to make a new room for Leonard, which they'd decided on, despite worries about Hitler and impending war – a long, narrow library under the roof, nicknamed Hedgehog Hall. The work coincided with their summer

The balcony was Leonard's last-minute idea when a new library was built for him in 1938.

sojourn, but Virginia seemed surprisingly unruffled by the disturbance. Halfway through the work, just as the new gable window had been installed, Leonard had what Virginia called 'the brilliant idea' of converting it into glass doors – with a balcony; she anticipated the pleasure of sitting there on a hot night and looking at the stars.

There were other luxuries: beds from Heal's and a Zeiss Ikon camera for Leonard (he developed and printed his photographs). Life was altogether becoming more comfortable for them – and for their guests. From the beginning she invited friends to stay, advising one that 'nightgowns are worn here'. Even before she had moved in to Monk's House she had been planning guests, urging Margaret Llewelyn Davies to come to sit in front of the fireplace with Leonard in one inglenook and herself in the other: 'It's time we had a good gossip.' Visitors were warned of the discomforts – especially when it rained. And it was bitterly cold. Frequent visitor Morgan Forster singed his trousers by standing too close to a 'Cozy Stove', commemorating it in verse. The main guest room had been a tiny space opposite the staircase between the kitchen and drawing room. When inviting Vita to stay, she had described it as a

View from the house down the garden that was Leonard's pride and joy.

cupboard room. It was to become the dining area, with fluted wooden columns each side of the entrance that were added in 1937.

Virginia often invited guests for tea. Diana Gardner, a young neighbour, remembered Virginia saying, as she offered teacakes and tea from a brown enamelled teapot, 'old-fashioned pots like these make the best tea.' Gladys Easdale, the mother of one of the Hogarth Young Poets, gave a detailed and admiring account of the 'tea set on a long refectory table, with purple lustreware, home-made bread and cakes, and honey from their five hives by the churchyard wall. There were crumpets too – these Mrs Woolf had specially bought to toast there and then herself because it was her fancy, she said, to do so as few, she continued, understood the pleasure of having crumpets for tea.'

The 'cool green' of the main room made her think of being underwater – which was precisely the effect that Virginia had intended when she painted it. Books lay on chairs, tables and stairs. Ripe apples lay everywhere.

As the guests were taken on a tour of the garden and the house, she remarked on the oddity of the new room built on: 'they have to come outside the house to get to it'. Then they returned to the living room and sat round the fragrant log fire and talked of ghosts and phantasms of the living, of poetry and accidents, of books and writers. 'Mrs Woolf excels as a talker and in making us all talk. She lights up with her own wit the plainest words.'

Though Virginia frequently issued invitations, she was ambivalent, often wishing guests gone when they arrived. She liked it when they came but loved it when they went: sometimes she longed for a house in a wood with a two-mile drive. There was continual conflict between her gregariousness and her desire to be alone; the conflict between society and solitude. Like Eleanor Pargiter sitting on the top deck of a London bus in *The Years*, who reflected that she 'liked coming back in October to the full stir of life after the summer was over', Virginia wanted to be back in London (and to travel on the top deck of the bus), but there was also often a jolt, the prospect of too many visitors, too many arrangements. At Monk's House she relished a weekend of no talking: 'never a person to be seen; the place to ourselves: the long hours.' What they both enjoyed was to 'sit, eat, play the gramophone, prop our feet up on the side of the fire and read endless books.'

Virginia passed through these water meadows on her walks.

Reading was ever a consolation, and a necessity, for her. She wrote once to Dame Ethel Smyth that her concept of heaven was 'one continuous unexhausted reading', describing the trance-like rapture that seized her every now and again since she was a girl. Indeed, the last book she thought of in the intervals of composing *Between the Acts* was a celebration of literature and the landscapes that had inspired it, of the writers and 'the views from their windows as they work'.

If they went out, there might just be the noise of the horses going down to the Brooks: not a voice, not a telephone. Virginia needed London for its streets and its stimulation. But she relied on the countryside and its isolation for calm and writing. She would go to her lodge across the garden: she had the regularity of a stockbroker, said Leonard, and would often work sitting in a chair with a board across her knees. She was thrilled with herself in 1933 when she managed to make herself a perfect writing board with pen tray attached. Leonard gave her an even better one with an ink well attached for Christmas the following year.

View across to Mount Caburn, the highest point in this part of Sussex.

She walked almost every day, sometimes over to Charleston, a six-mile walk including a steep hill (she had stamina), along favoured routes, often by the river, but searching out new ones too. She once wrote to Ethel about a particularly lovely discovery, a valley with 'silver sheep clustering on the sides, hares leaping from my foot, and great horses slowly dragging wagons like shaggy sea monsters – but corn was dripping instead of seaweed.' She gloried in the countryside, ever sensitive to her surroundings but also teasing out a plot or a character, writing the sentences in her head. The actor Dirk Bogarde, who lived nearby as a child, recalled seeing her 'marching about the water meadows quite often', apparently singing to herself. Leonard thought she spent most of her waking day writing – whether on her knee, on her desk or on the Downs.

Sussex was the place where she could slow her pace, watch the natural things in life – and practise her words. As she watched rooks 'beating up against the wind' she spent a few lines in her diary trying to convey this scene and concluding it was impossible to adequately describe something that felt so elemental. This was what she used her diary for – not just as a record or a way of releasing her emotions, but as a place to explore her ideas and techniques. She often examined her responses to sights and sounds. This was mainly only possible in the stillness of Rodmell. 'Now and again I feel my mind take shape, like a cloud with the sun on it . . . I wait peacefully for another to form.'

She made nature notes – a kingfisher, two cormorants rising from the marsh, the stooks of corn, cattle galloping, the clouds, a weasel, the rare sight of two foxes on her birthday walk in 1930 – finding the poetry of Gerard Manley Hopkins suited her perfectly at this time for its appreciation of nature and lyrical word combinations. 'The twig carrying has begun,' she reported one March – a sentence echoed in her last book; the snake trying to swallow a toad, seen on a walk with Leonard in September 1935, appears there too.

There were drawbacks to Rodmell, of course, though much depended on her mood. The church bells, for example, infuriated her on occasion, and the woman who owned the house on the other side of the path to the church kept spaniels – very vocal ones. On a more serious level, there was recurrent anxiety about incomers. Inconsistent though it might be for these most distinguished of writers who had just arrived, she abhorred the idea of other literary figures taking up residence in Rodmell. But they were not the only ones attracted. The fact was, surprisingly, that in the 1920s Rodmell was suffering from the country-cottage syndrome: 'Rich people wanting week end cottages buy up the old peasants' houses for fabulous sums,' she noted. Just as today the young leave villages for work and for pleasure, so the same was happening in Rodmell then.

And there was another cloud on the horizon: a cement works, plundering the chalk of the hill that their cherished former home nestled under, and right in the line of vision from the garden writing room. They were both furious at the drive to produce cement, 'of which England has already more than she can use'. Virginia documented the development, month by month and with increasing hyperbole. Soon there were three iron sheds – 'glaring monstrosities' – 'literally' the size of St Paul's, Westminster Abbey, the Albert Hall. There was no respite even at night, because of the lights. 'Down and marsh murdered inch by inch,' she despaired.

The view she 'always swore was eternal and incorruptible' ruined. She raged and often woke at night in misery.

A trip to Greece restored her equanimity: a postcard to Julian lists the birds (eagles, bee-eaters, blue thrushes) as well as the ruins, temples and statues; and she dallied with the idea of moving the Hogarth Press to Crete. It was the best holiday she'd had for years. But back at home, there were other threats. Virginia discovered that the man who had bought Southease Farm was starting a pony racecourse, with stable and a stand; then there was the prospect of a goat farm on a hill near Northease. She worried at the rumours about building sixty workmen's cottages on the farm for sale at the top of the village – but there was a reprieve as in the end the farm was bought by a horse-breeder. Council houses were built on Mill Lane later, and a hideous house built at the top of Mill Hill, 'Hancock's Horror'. (She later had to be polite to the owner as he was the Labour candidate for Lewes and came to party meetings in Monk's House.)

Despite the house-building this was, she declared time and again, still the loveliest countryside in the world, with corn ripening and yellow butterflies. However, in May 1928, they were in turmoil. From Virginia's garden workroom the view was across a strip of flat land next to their garden that fell steeply into Pound Croft Field. Both field and terrace were about to be bought for building. There had been intermittent anxiety about this patch of land: in the early days, they had considered buying the meadow but had decided they already had more land than they wanted. This time Leonard was inclined to sell and go, and Virginia started looking at adverts for houses in Dorset and East Anglia.

Calamity was averted as that summer, after several efforts, Leonard managed to purchase the land. Their view was preserved, and Virginia noted a change in her feelings about Rodmell, as she thought she could now 'dig' herself in. Leonard installed on the terrace a dew pond like the ones on the Downs. He rented out the field to the local farmer who had used it for grazing; the terrace became the bowling green, to be the site of many contests between Leonard and Virginia, mostly won by Leonard to Virginia's chagrin.

Whenever faced with one of these threats – and even when not – she indulged in a favourite pastime: house-hunting. As early as 1923, she had been restless,

Virginia's nephew Quentin Bell watching his half-sister Angelica bowling on the terrace by the writing lodge.

wanting to explore Sussex to find a perfect house. She said, 'There's nothing I enjoy more than looking for houses, and imagining that I am going to find the very thing.' There was, as she'd told Vanessa when she bought Charleston, 'nothing in the world' as exciting as a new house. It was an interest Leonard shared. So they went to look at a farm in the meadows near the village of Ripe. They considered a house in Arundel. They paced out a meadow with a wonderful view, 'but L says we are too old to build a house.' In 1925, Leonard had briefly contemplated a chicken farm, when the Rodmell cottage of poet Edward Shanks became available (he had left the village, to the relief of Virginia who wanted to avoid the literary scene when in Sussex). Later Lime Kiln Farm near Selmeston, a Tudor house with small 'eyebrowed' windows, was on the viewing list, but it was very unappealing with its mildewed carpets and sticky walls, and there was also a house in Southease, with its pretty round-towered church, under consideration for a short time.

Laughton Place, near Glynde, looked promising. A sixteenth-century brick tower, the only part remaining of a splendid mansion with terracotta decoration, erected by Sir William Pelham, who had the distinction of attending Henry VIII at the Field of the Cloth of Gold, scene of Henry's fortnight-long friendship summit with Francis I of France. By 1600 the home had been abandoned by the family, driven by the damp to build on higher ground, though a later Pelham did incorporate the tower into a charming Gothic-style farmhouse. On a sunny September morning in 1927, when it was for sale, Vita and Virginia drove over to see it. Virginia, who broke in to explore, was excited at the peaceful location and what seemed like endless old rooms. She and Leonard were full of enthusiasm and wrote to ask if they could buy it. But on closer investigation of the interior – 'unspeakably dreary; all patched & spoilt; with grained & grey paper; a sodden garden' – they pulled out. Leonard commented to Virginia over the disappointment about Laughton Place that 'the strange thing is that we always come to the same opinion about things,' a remark that she cherished. The new owner pulled down the farmhouse wings, leaving only the tower – and in 1978 the Landmark Trust bought it and rescued it from dilapidation.

A month later, they were taken by Amberley, a pretty village between water meadows and downs, that they came across on a motor trip and thought of buying a house there, and they also pondered on Wilmington, near Alfriston. There were bursts of house-hunting throughout, followed by the realization that Monk's House and Rodmell were lovely enough to suspend searching. On returning after one such expedition, Virginia found, unexpectedly, that she appreciated it anew: the view from the house; the lily that had sprung four flowers.

Leonard's passion for flowers never abated. There was another fallout in 1939 when yet another 'Crystal Palace' greenhouse, with boilers, for the exotic plants Leonard loved to grow was being erected. Seeing Virginia's reaction that morning, he went straight out and gave instructions for it to be taken down again. A compromise was reached, and Leonard got his greenhouse. The arguments never lasted long. On one occasion, she crept into Leonard's bed to make up a 'sham quarrel'. On another, he bought her a blue glass jug to make up for being cross with her when she slapped his nose with a bunch of sweet peas. And what was striking was how she could still look out of the window at Leonard working in the garden or up a ladder pruning a tree and, as she said, catch her breath at how handsome he was: 'my heart stood still with pride that he ever married me.' A couple of years earlier, Virginia had pondered on how life might have been if she had married

Lytton, and concluded that she would never have written as much as she had done. 'Leonard may be severe, but he stimulates. Anything is possible with him.'

They were then living more and more at Monk's House, in their customary state of 'ramshackle informality'. During the 1930s, their visits had become more frequent, and fortnightly weekends had expanded into stays from Thursday evening until Monday morning, though Virginia had been a trifle ambivalent about finding her social London life curtailed. But she noted approvingly in March 1940 that it was the first time she had properly seen spring in the country since 1914 at Asheham. More alterations were being considered: that year, while Virginia was sleeping in Leonard's room during a period of ill health (the outdoor entrance to hers had disadvantages), they debated turning this into her bedroom with 'a bathroom in a cupboard'.

Their move to live there full-time had been forced on them when 37 Mecklenburgh Square suffered bomb damage. All the furniture and archives and thousands of books from there had to be stored in rooms rented around Rodmell, as well as in Monk's House, which became unbelievably cluttered. Her great-nephew Julian, Quentin's son, wrote of the 'great piles of books, a maze of waist-high piles to be negotiated every time you crossed a room. Interspersed with manuscripts, magazines, ashtrays, sometimes pets.' Her life inevitably had become less comfortable, less sociable, more circumscribed.

Virginia did become more involved in the community, though she still had mixed feelings about Rodmell. The local Labour Party meetings took place in their house. She allowed herself to be nominated by Annie, her former housekeeper, as treasurer of the Women's Institute, and found speakers for the WI. She herself gave a hilarious talk on the Dreadnought Hoax.

Her work schedule continued unabated. She struggled with the biography of Roger Fry, and the unfamiliar constraint of facts, but *Pointz Hall* provided the occasional welcome relief as she stole time from her research. She'd had the first idea in the spring of 1938. Recounting the events of a summer's night and set in 'a remote village in the very heart of England', it echoes much of Rodmell, especially

Springtime in the orchard.

the village pageant representing a satirical version of the history of England. She was inspired by Mrs Ebbs, the rector's wife, who directed the annual village fete and plays: the gardener Percy's daughter Marie starred in one, playing Puck in *A Midsummer Night's Dream.* Pointz Hall itself might have been inspired by the Elizabethan manor house at Glynde near Glyndebourne (visited in 1934 and 1935) or Firle Place. But there were many aspects of Monk's House and its garden that feature, such as the Glazebrook paintings and the fishpond. Virginia was buoyant, enjoying the writing, though the build-up to war – never explicit – was the constant background.

One day, as she was in her writing lodge, she looked out of the window and wondered if instead of writing her diary she should just be looking at the sunset. She captured the very stillness of that moment, Leonard collecting apples, the cows grazing, pear tree laden – but all noted and set against the 'cadaverous twanging in the sky' of German bombers heading towards London.

Just before war had been declared, Virginia had summoned Leonard to hear one of Hitler's speeches on the radio. Leonard, as he recounts at the end of his third volume of his autobiography *Downhill All The Way* (published in 1967) refused to listen, continuing to plant irises under the apple tree, reflecting, at the time of writing, that they were still blooming twenty-one years after Hitler's death.

The war in some ways seemed closer than ever here. There was a very real prospect of invasion and, as Rodmell was so close to the coast, Leonard laid in a stock of petrol so they could asphyxiate themselves in the garage. This threat was hanging over them, but just as real to Virginia was the agonizing about loss of friendship, after a letter to Elizabeth Bowen had been unanswered. (It echoed earlier angst over Rebecca West, who, it turned out, had been ill.) Contact was re-established leading to a valued reunion in London and a walk from Mecklenburgh Square through Temple and up Thames Street to the Tower 'talking talking'.

One October night in 1940 Leonard and Virginia went on to the terrace under a night sky with 'trinkets of stars sprinkled and glittering' to see Mount Caburn 'crowned with what looked like a settled moth'. It was a Messerschmitt, shot down three days before. There were continued sightings of German planes circling overhead when playing bowls, dropping bombs over Lewes while they lay flat on

The pots in the flower garden were bought by Leonard and Virginia.

their faces, hands behind their heads; all her senses were on the alert: 'a horse neighed on the marsh.' And yet she wrote often of the peacefulness and freedom of being at Monk's House, of life contracting to the village radius – no servant, being able to dine when they liked, the pleasures of needlework. They were living near the bone, as she put it. 'I think we've mastered life rather competently.'

But the New Year dawned with increasing despair about raids on London: '8 of my city churches gone'. On a visit to London that January she wandered 'in the desolate ruins of my old squares.' The demolition of 52 Tavistock Square had now happened – but accomplished by a bomb. The panels painted by Vanessa and Duncan could be seen hanging and broken.

In Rodmell she attended fire drills, first-aid lectures and WI meetings, she cycled to Lewes to do her shopping, packing provisions into the basket in front.

But there was no substitute for the concerts, the exhibitions, the easy meetings over tea with friends in London, even in wartime. In February, Elizabeth Bowen came to stay at Monk's House, one of Virginia's last visitors. Years later, she recollected Virginia's 'capacity for joy' and in particular the last day she saw her, 'I remember her kneeling back on the floor – we were tacking away, mending a torn Spanish curtain in the house – and she sat back on her heels and put her head back in a patch of sun, early spring sun. Then she laughed in the consuming, choking, delightful, hooting way. And that is what has remained with me.'

Ten days later, Virginia finished *Pointz Hall!*, changing its title to *Between the Acts*, and gave the manuscript to Leonard. But as so often before, the completion of it brought on terrible anxieties. Leonard could see the warning signs, but unusually, she would not retire to bed. Instead she chose more physical activity – which included, surprisingly, as a neighbour making a delivery discovered, washing the floor.

On 18 March, Leonard met her coming back to the house, soaking wet: she said she had fallen into a brook. Her mood became worse and she was more fragile. She wrote to John Lehmann that her book could not be published, that it was 'too silly and trivial'.

Leonard took her to see the doctor Octavia Wilberforce, who wrote to a friend of her last conversation with Virginia about how she felt she had lost the art of writing. She talked bitterly: 'I'm buried down here – I've not the stimulation of seeing people.' It was the society versus solitude axis again, but the balance in these times of war, when their London home had gone, was out of kilter.

On Friday 28 March, she did some dusting: 'I'd never known her want to do any housework with me before,' said Louie, the housekeeper. In the late morning she left home by the garden gate and walked through the Brooks towards the river. When Leonard came back to the house at lunchtime he found two letters on the table in the sitting room, one to him and one to Vanessa. His began with her conviction that she was going mad again and ended 'Two people could not have been happier than we have been.' He ran to Percy's house – Marie, his daughter, remembers it: 'He looked haunted. I shall never forget his face when he burst into the room' – and sent him to fetch the local constable. He ran to the river, and found Virginia's walking stick. But the frantic searches revealed nothing. They could only wait.

The River Ouse was a pleasant, meandering river until it was widened and embanked with rocks in the 1960s to prevent repeated flooding.

A note Leonard wrote at this time and found among his papers after he died said 'I know that V will not come across the garden from the lodge, and yet I look in that direction for her. I know that she is drowned and yet I listen for her to come in at the door. I know it is the last page & yet I turn it over.'

Three weeks later, a group of teenagers, cycling from Lewes to Seaford, stopped by Asheham to have their lunch in a field near the cement works and river. They saw what they thought was a log floating, then one of the boys waded out to it and overturned it with a stick shouting 'It's a woman. A woman in a fur coat.'

The cremation took place on 21 April in Brighton, with only Leonard in attendance. He buried Virginia's ashes under the interlaced elms, Leonard and Virginia. He had a plaque made with the last words of *The Waves*: 'Against you I will fling myself, unvanquished and unyielding, O Death!' As Leonard wrote in the last volume of his autobiography, *The Journey Not the Arrival Matters*: 'In the first week of January 1943, in a great gale, one of the elms was blown down.'

# The Legacy

*'What cuts the deepest channels in our lives are the different houses in which we live'*

---

Monk's House remained Leonard's home, but he needed a base in London for his work at Hogarth Press. At the end of 1941, he poignantly returned to his and Virginia's first home, Clifford's Inn, which had been rebuilt as a block of service flats, before deciding that he would prefer to make do in their bombed-out house in Mecklenburgh Square, where he patched together three rooms. Eventually, he moved to 24 Victoria Square, a surprisingly quiet enclave two minutes from Victoria station. But his heart was in Monk's House and Rodmell, and he stayed on there, with Louie remaining as his housekeeper.

His first priority after Virginia's death was to bring out *Between the Acts*, which appeared in July 1941, and increasingly his days were taken up with the afterlife of Virginia. She had left two last letters for Leonard. It seems likely that the one he had found in the house, dated Tuesday, was written ten days before her death, the day Leonard had met her in a drenched state. The other letter was in her writing lodge, and probably written on the morning of the day she died: the last words were 'Will you destroy all my papers.'

Leonard did not. Virginia herself would surely not have wanted them discarded. She had sometimes spoken to her diary about its future purpose, imagining 'old Virginia' looking back over her life, thinking of their use for a memoir, and speculating on what Leonard might do with her diaries if she died first: she knew

This bust of Virginia in Monk's House garden is a copy of the 1931 original by Stephen Tomlin. The eyes are unfinished because she couldn't bear to continue the sittings.

that there was enough for 'a little book' in them. He had, she wrote in 1927, picked up that year's journal and looked at her handwriting, saying 'Lord save him if I died first & he had to read through these.'

Leonard arranged for her diaries to be transcribed and typed. The originals were placed in his bank in Lewes, while he kept a transcript at home. He would himself edit a selection of extracts from the twenty-six volumes for *A Writer's Diary*, published in 1953, as well as editing several collections of her essays. Some years later, he asked Vanessa's son, Quentin, by then an academic (as well as author and artist), to write Virginia's biography. At first Quentin refused, but when he agreed to a second request in 1966, Leonard gave him the carbon copies of the diary typescripts, which, it turned out, were in tatters, because bits had been cut out of the carbons for the *Writer's Diary*. When this omission was pointed out, Leonard put the remnants he'd used in a foolscap envelope and sent it to Quentin, saying that now he had the complete text!

Quentin's wife, Anne Olivier Bell, well trained as a researcher, reconstructed the text by typing out all the copies, laboriously reinserting the excised portions after comparison with the published *Writer's Diary*. After that, she drew up a chronological card system for all the references, against which everything was checked: 'But somehow our marriage survived, the biography was written, and was perhaps none the worse for being factually accurate.' *Virginia Woolf: A Biography* was published in two volumes in 1972.

In due course, Anne Olivier Bell edited the five volumes of diaries (with, as one might expect from the above, excellent footnotes). The last volume appeared in 1984. Nigel Nicolson, son of Vita Sackville-West and Harold Nicolson, who'd known Virginia since childhood, took charge of Virginia's letters, which appeared in six volumes between 1975 and 1980. The diaries themselves Leonard had agreed in 1957 to sell to American book dealers, Frances Hamill and Marjorie Barker, after finding no interest in her papers from any English library. The conditions were that he was paid then; that he retained them during his lifetime; and that they went to a major public archive. They are now in the Berg Collection of the New York Public Library.

Long before these publications, Leonard was receiving approaches from academics and researchers. The first study in English, *Virginia Woolf: a Critical*

*Memoir* by Winifred Holtby (also author of the novel *South Riding*) had appeared in 1932. After Virginia's death, interest grew and grew. Leonard dealt conscientiously and courteously with requests, responding to all and co-operating with some. He safeguarded her copyright, though did not necessarily charge a fee. In 1962 the playwright Edward Albee asked permission of Leonard to use his wife's name in *Who's Afraid of Virginia Woolf?* – which catapulted recognition of her name, if not her works, to an immeasurably wider audience. Leonard almost always agreed to meet the procession of applicants. He was the keeper of his wife's flame.

Eventually there were also approaches to obtain the original manuscripts of everything she had written. The reason that these are now mostly in America is because Leonard was impressed by the interest and commitment there to make everything available to students. Karen Kukil, Curator of Special Collections at Smith College, Massachusetts, remarked in her presentation to the 2016 International Virginia Woolf Conference on the prevalence of Virginia Woolf on the curriculum in American universities as far back as the 1920s.

Now Virginia Woolf appears on syllabuses all over the world, and her books are translated into almost every language, sometimes by authors eminent in their own right; for example, Argentinian novelist Jorge Luis Borges translated *A Room of One's Own*. She is studied in prisons: crime correspondent and author Duncan Campbell recounts his friendship with armed bank robber Bobby King, who had studied Virginia Woolf in his progress towards an Open University MA. When Duncan met him one evening at a London pub he was reading *To the Lighthouse* while he waited; when Duncan mentioned this to another ex-convict with an OU degree, his immediate response was 'not her best'.

There are classes and summer courses – at Cambridge University, for example (her politics in 2018, her gardens in 2019) – and international conferences on Virginia Woolf are held at universities, often in America, sometimes in Britain (three in a row from 2016 to 2018 in Leeds, Reading and Canterbury) and occasionally in Asia. The panoply of papers presented covers a dazzling array of aspects of her life and works from straightforward to frankly esoteric. In the programme at the Leeds Trinity University 2016 conference, for example,

*To the Lighthouse* was subjected to examination from the point of view of 'Quantum Realism' and also of '(Un)Productive (Non)Motherhood: Affective Femininity'.

Academic interest led, in 1973, to the launch of a newsletter, the *Virginia Woolf Miscellany*, a forum for reviews, reminiscences, notes and queries, as a resource for academics and ordinary readers alike. On the back of that, a Virginia Woolf Society was formed in America in 1976; the Virginia Woolf Society in England followed in 1998, publishing the *Virginia Woolf Bulletin* three times a year, including a column, 'Virginia Woolf Today', which includes allusions in reviews, novels, articles and broadcasts – they occur almost daily.

Books of all sorts, using Virginia Woolf as the starting point, have been published: Virginia Woolf and the clergy; and the politics of language; and nature; and reality. The British Library has over 3,000 titles, many of them spin-offs, such as *To the River: A Journey Beneath the Surface*, a meditation on Woolf and the River Ouse by Olivia Laing, who walked from its source to the sea. A children's

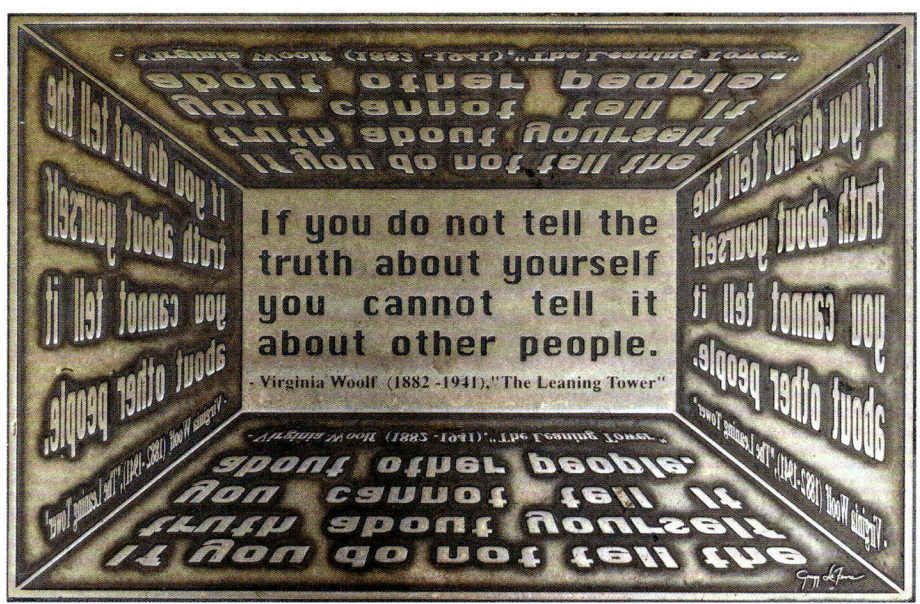

One of many memorials to Virginia, this bronze plaque was among the 96 embedded in the pavement of New York's E 41st Street, called 'Library Walk'.

book, *Virginia Wolf*, by Kyo Maclear and Isabelle Arsenault (the blurb reads: 'One day my sister Virginia woke up feeling wolfish. She made wolf sounds and did strange things. . .') captures well the 'atmosphere of tense thundery gloom' that Vanessa remembered about Virginia as a child. Maggie Gee's *Virginia Woolf in Manhattan* brings her back to life in a comedy spanning New York and Istanbul. There's even a book on Mitz: *The Marmoset of Bloomsbury*.

Her own novels are resurrected in surprising ways. A musical version of *Orlando* was planned as early as 1952, though nothing came of that plan, and the story was famously made into the 1992 film by Sally Potter starring Tilda Swinton. There have been many adaptations of *The Waves* on radio, and

This 2006 stamp, celebrating the National Portrait Gallery, shows the George Charles Beresford portrait of Virginia.

on stage, including a 1990 musical in New York; in 1993 *Mrs Dalloway* became a chamber opera, and also inspired *The Hours* by Michael Cunningham, the novel that led to the 2002 film based on the effect of *Mrs Dalloway* on the lives of three women of different generations (one being Virginia Woolf). In 2017, the Institute of Psychoanalysis held a screening of *The Hours* as a curtain-raiser for discussions on her mental condition (and her hatred of the medical profession) and how her experimental writing style, the stream of consciousness, coincided with the free association of the processes of psychology.

Particularly innovative was the ballet *Woolf Works*, first staged at the Royal Opera House in 2015 and again in 2017. It won the Critics' Circle Award for best classic choreography, and the Olivier award for best new production. Introduced by the only recording of her voice, the only surviving part of her BBC talk in a

The award-winning ballet *Woolf Works* was first presented at the Royal Opera House in 2015, with a score by innovative composer Max Richter.

series called Words Fail Me, broadcast in 1937 ('she talks about words almost as if they are living creatures.' said Max Richter, composer of the music), the ballet is in three parts: the first, 'I Now, I Then', based on *Mrs Dalloway*; the second, 'Beginnings', on *Orlando*; and the third, 'Tuesday', on *The Waves*. Its choreographer, Wayne MacGregor, said 'What I get over and over again when I read Woolf is the absolute brilliance about being able to describe and to hold on to this really varied and multi-dimensional life that we all lead.' Max Richter had been 'obsessively' drawn to Virginia's writing in his early twenties and called his involvement 'a voyage of discovery', describing the extraordinary sense of movement in *Mrs Dalloway*, 'the multiplicity of tempos' that he translated into the music, using orchestral and electronic music along with field recordings such as the striking of Big Ben to convey 'the pulse of the city, clocks ticking, all the characters traversing London'. *Orlando* was 'an extraordinary journey spanning hundreds of years, changing of genders, all sorts of travelling'. The theme of transformation 'lends itself to a variation form. It's almost like putting grit in the oyster to make the pearl. It's recognizable, but subtly altered.'

Her work and life has provided inspiration for music (there's a website devoted entirely to this subject: virginiawoolfmusic.wp.st-andrews.ac.uk); for clothes (Burberry's 2016 fashion show was inspired by *Orlando*, and one American website has over 300 teeshirts and baby bodysuits with images or quotes); for a publishing imprint: Hogarth is a joint transatlantic project by Chatto & Windus and Crown – and its latest manifestation is a fiction list overseen by *Sex and the City*'s Sarah Jane Parker. Inevitably, there has also been satire: comic novelist Sue Limb has written five series of a spoof on Bloomsbury called *Gloomsbury* for BBC Radio 4. (Ginny and Lionel Fox are the main characters, along with Vera Sackville-Vest and Henry Mickleton.)

The capacity of Virginia Woolf to inspire and energize is noticeable in the frequency of her references in all sorts of media. The singer Emeli Sandé has a tattoo in homage on her left arm: *Un Cuartro Proprio*, Spanish for *A Room of One's Own*. Virginia has been given her own Facebook page. She was even on Twitter for a year from July 2014, courtesy of a fan who tweeted daily entries from her diary. And there are so many blogs – even about her use of apostrophes.

There are more tangible tributes to her, some made in her lifetime: portraits by Vanessa; photographs by Gisèle Freund and Man Ray. In 1931 she posed unwillingly for a bust by Stephen Tomlin: it was not entirely completed because Virginia could not bear to continue the sittings, her customary fear of being scrutinized and mocked coming to the fore. (In 2004, the Virginia Woolf Society unveiled a copy of this bust on a plinth of Portland stone in the corner of Tavistock Square.) Most quirky was Boris Anrep's marble mosaic at the top of the entrance flight of stairs to the National Gallery installed in 1933: in The Awakening of the Muses, Clio, the muse of history, is represented as Virginia, pen in hand. In

The 2018 plaque marking 52 Tavistock Square on the wall of the Tavistock Hotel.

Richmond there is to be a bronze sculpture of Virginia sitting on a bench at the riverside. Cheryl Robson of arts and education charity Aurora Metro started a campaign for this in 2016, and in the spring of 2018 planning permission was granted.

There are blue plaques, of course, in Kensington, Richmond and Gordon Square: 22 Hyde Park Gate has the distinction of being the only house with three, celebrating Virginia, Vanessa and Leslie. 46 Gordon Square actually has a plaque for Maynard Keynes on it, as he lived there too; at 50 is the plaque to the Bloomsbury Group. And in June 2018, members of a theatre company in the guise of Virginia, Lytton, and other members of the Bloomsbury Group were perambulating through Gordon Square on Open Garden Squares weekend practising for *The Memoir Club*, a promenade theatre show to be staged at that year's Bloomsbury Festival.

In 2018, a new plaque was placed by the Virginia Woolf Society on the wall of Tavistock Hotel, which now occupies the south side of Tavistock Square: 52, Virginia and Leonard's home for fifteen years, had stood on the site of the entrance. Naturally, the Tavistock Hotel has a bar called after her, The Woolf and Whistle (its toilets papered with titles and images of Virginia). Its sister hotel, The Bloomsbury in Great Russell Street, has the Dalloway Terrace restaurant.

But what of her other homes? Talland House is now stranded like a beached whale on the slopes of St Ives among modern villas with sharp-pointed roofs and flats with glass balconies, its garden nibbled away over the years by car parks and buildings. A worldwide campaign from lovers of Virginia Woolf failed to stop planning permission being granted for a block of flats that would obscure

# THE LEGACY

This picture was used in the campaign to raise funds for a bronze statue of Virginia to be unveiled by the river in Richmond in 2019.

the emblematic view of the Godrevy lighthouse, though it has not yet been built. Talland House as it was exists only in Virginia's memories and fiction.

22 Hyde Park Gate was run for thirty years as a hotel from 1943, and is now divided into flats – for a while, one of them was a bed-and-breakfast favoured by Woolf fans. 46 Gordon Square is now, along with its neighbours in the terrace, home to the School of Arts of Birkbeck College, part of the University of London. It is open for visits during Open House, the festival of architecture giving free access to buildings over one September weekend each year. In Fitzroy Square, an elegant and pedestrianized area restored to the original Adam design, 29 is the premises of a practice of chartered accountants.

Hogarth House, and its neighbour Suffield House, served almost a century as offices, latterly as a single business centre. In 2012 it was bought by developer Jeremy Richardson of Berwick Hill. He had experience in conversions of Georgian offices in Queen Anne's Gate for residential use, and enlisted the help of Jonathan Carey of Donald Insall Associates, architects and historic buildings consultant (previous jobs included restoration of Windsor Castle after the fire in 1992), who did a great deal of detective work, finding evidence of the separation into two houses. Between them, Richardson and Carey persuaded

The conservatory on the side of Monk's House, enveloping the main entrance, replaced Leonard's greenhouses and was filled with his delicate plants.

the local conservation officer, who wanted this as a single residence, that it could legitimately be turned back into the two houses of the Woolfs' time. The painstaking restoration began in January 2016, with the exquisite panelling of the drawing room, its large squares ornamented by shells and fleur-de-lys gently uncovered, the central staircase Leonard so admired ingeniously moved and resurrected in the original Hogarth House. The view of the pagoda at Kew Gardens from the upstairs rooms, fondly remembered by Virginia, has been obscured by new buildings, but the gracious proportions of the house remain. By the autumn of 2017, it was ready to go on the market as two houses – named Leonard and Virginia – at £3.75 million each.

Asheham, 'extraordinarily romantic' in Leonard's view, did not fare so well. The cement sheds so loathed by Virginia were demolished in 1978, and landfill restored Iford Hill. The house itself, increasingly redundant and derelict, was finally, despite a campaign to save it, demolished in 1994 by the cement company that owned it after the local council turned down plans to relocate it. Compensation paid to East Sussex County Council was partly used to set up the Asham Literary Endowment Trust, which ran a biennial short story competition.

The home that does happily remain is Monk's House in Rodmell. It has changed a little since Virginia's day. Following on from Leonard's enthusiasm for greenhouses, there is now attached to the side of the house, encasing the door they used, a large conservatory, which Leonard filled with plants. The garden lodge was doubled in size, so that half could be used as a studio by artist Trekkie Parsons.

Trekkie Parsons, close companion of Leonard in his later years, in the greenhouse in Monk's House.

Trekkie Parsons was the younger sister of Alice Ritchie, who had been Hogarth Press's sales representative in the 1920s. When Alice was dying of cancer in 1941, Leonard visited her several times as she was staying at Trekkie's home in Victoria Square, though he didn't meet Trekkie until 1942, after Alice's death. Over time, their relationship became very close and though she stayed with her husband, Ian Parsons, she spent much time with Leonard at Monk's House, a platonic but deeply affectionate relationship.

Ian Parsons, a publisher with Chatto & Windus, had long been hopeful of linking with Hogarth Press. In 1946, when Leonard's partner at Hogarth, John Lehmann, quarrelled with him, Leonard bought back his share and amalgamated Hogarth Press with Chatto & Windus. He remained active in Hogarth Press,

A prizewinning display at the summer show of Rodmell Horticultural and Allotment Society, co-founded by Leonard in 1940.

looking in once a week, reading manuscripts and meeting authors for almost all of the rest of his life.

Throughout the 1960s he wrote his five-volume autobiography, including the award-winning third volume *Beginning Again*, published in 1964. This principally covered the years 1911 to 1918, though when writing about the early days of their marriage, he digressed from the chronology to expound upon Monk's House and its importance in their lives: 'What cuts the deepest channels in our lives are the different houses in which we live.' He endured interviews, including with Malcolm Muggeridge and with Karl Miller, editor of *The Listener*, for BBC's Third Programme in 1967, when Leonard asserted that *The Waves* was the only great novel she wrote. 'At last she got to the method which enabled her to say exactly what she wanted to say.' He felt she did that in *Between the Acts* too. *The Years*, he said was her worst book but 'a bestseller [he sighed] both in America and here'.

Though an award-winning author, Leonard may well have been a great deal prouder of the accolade he received in 1968 at the summer show of the Rodmell Horticultural and Allotment Society, where, with the help of his new gardener,

# THE LEGACY

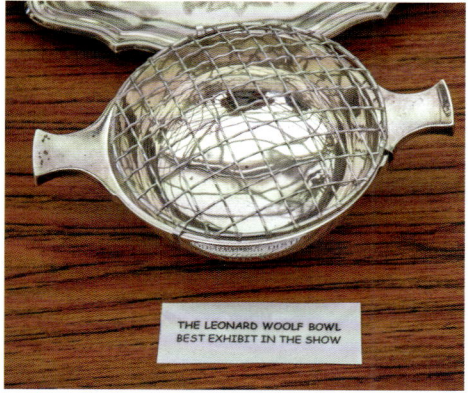

Leonard's role in setting up the Rodmell Horticultural Society is marked by this trophy.

More prizewinners in the vegetable category.

Vout Van der Keift, he won six firsts, all for vegetables. He had co-founded the Society in 1940 with its purpose of improving the wartime diet. The first recorded committee meeting was on 23 October at Monk's House, chaired by Leonard. In 1943 he was re-elected as President and Treasurer (he signed all AGM minutes until 1967). 1946 saw the first Vegetable and Flower Show: Leonard is commemorated still in the Leonard Woolf Bowl, engraved with the dates he was president, 1940–69. Rodmell Horticultural Society's summer show is held every August with prizes for everything from chutney to cherry tomatoes. All is laid out neatly on tables in the big tent, with music from a band, a bicycle ice-cream seller and a coconut shy.

Fittingly, he won awards every year and, proud of his garden as he was, he also opened it one day every year for charity under the National Gardens Scheme from 1950 until 1969. Most of the vegetable garden behind its hawthorn hedge has been turned into allotments for the villagers, something he would have approved of.

He was also, at different times, treasurer of the cricket club, chairman of Rodmell Parish Council, and school manager: he used to give the pupils at the school, across the lane from the church, baskets of apples as an incentive to prevent them climbing over to scrump apples. He was embedded in the life of Rodmell in a way that Virginia never was, despite her affection for Monk's House and her love of the Sussex countryside. But she and Leonard would certainly have rejoiced at the designation of the South Downs as the most recent National Park in 2011, so at last it is protected from the development that Virginia and Leonard had so abhorred.

Leonard had a stroke in 1969, a day after showing visitors round the garden on its annual open day, and it was largely thanks to Louie's devoted attendance, as well as help from Trekkie and other friends, that he was able to live out his last days at Monk's House, where he died on 14 August. Leonard had bequeathed to Louie the cottage that was her home, but perhaps it had too many memories – she left Rodmell and went to live in Seaford. In 2002, after her death, Virginia's walking stick, which Leonard had given to her, was sold to an American bidder and is now in New York Public Library (an image can be seen on its website).

Leonard's ashes were buried under the remaining elm tree (later felled because of Dutch Elm Disease). Monk's House was left to Trekkie who, three years later, sold the whole property including the two village cottages to the University of Sussex, donating all Leonard's papers (known as the Monk's House Papers) as well. (In his last few years, Leonard had been friendly with Vice Chancellor and Professor of History Asa Briggs.) For some years the house was used by visiting academics. But in 1980, largely as a result of a campaign headed by Nigel Nicolson, Monk's House was bought by the National Trust, who for several years let out a studio flat over what was the garage, the room where Leonard used to work, giving guests the chance to experience the garden alone.

The house has been restored as much as possible, in paint scheme and furniture, to the days when the Woolfs lived there. The walls of the living room, painted white in Trekkie's time, have been returned to Virginia's favourite green. There is a table tiled by Duncan and a firescreen designed by Duncan, as well as a table made at the Omega Workshops under Roger Fry's supervision. A favourite snug armchair of Virginia's, covered with fabric designed by Vanessa, stands by the fire on one side, on the other the mahogany, button-backed red chair that had belonged to Leslie Stephen and which was used by Leonard.

One way the house differs from Virginia's time is in its tidiness. What visitors to the house always noted, apart from the profusion of bowls of apples in autumn,

# THE LEGACY

The Monk's House vegetable garden has now, fittingly, been turned into allotments for the villagers.

were the piles of books everywhere, on tables, on the floor, on the edge of the stairs. The entirety of the library – 4,000 books – was sold after Leonard's death and is now at Washington State University, with an online catalogue. The volumes of the Arden Shakespeare, in Virginia's bedroom, each covered in brightly coloured paper, are the only ones of hers that remain, because they and the delicate green bookcase they are in, had been given to a friend, Lady Lintott. After her death her children donated it to the National Trust in 2011.

## THE LEGACY

The garden is being restored as much as possible to Leonard's planting scheme, meticulously noted in his records, among the half walls, maze-like, and the brick paths, laid by Leonard. Miranda, their treasured statue, surveys the bowling terrace (a bucket of bowls stands ready to be played). In April 2018, Percy Bartholomew's daughter, Marie Bartholomew, led a group round the garden in one of her monthly tours, remarking wryly that she has been dubbed 'The Living Link'. Her stories of the original planting she knew as a child in the late 1930s, of the bee swarms (her job was to go and identify the spot where they had landed) and her particular affection for Leonard (Virginia was 'remote') gave listeners an invaluable insight into the life of the house as well as the garden.

One can still walk down through the water meadows, run through with rivulets and ditches, to the River Ouse, less picturesque than in Virginia's day since it was widened and contained by high banks of rocks to prevent flooding, but one can walk along to Southease, as she did. Rodmell no longer has the forge that, even in 1991, employed five blacksmiths, and the neighbouring garage, from which Leonard bought his petrol, has now gone. But the village community thrives and the Abergavenny Arms, where Virginia sometimes collected her ham, is still in business at the crossroads.

At Monk's House, the elm trees Leonard and Virginia have long gone. The plaque that marked Virginia's ashes has been moved to a wall at the centre of the garden by the fishpond. On one end of the wall is a cast of Stephen Tomlin's bust of Virginia. At the other, the head and shoulders of Leonard, as created in 1968 by Charlotte Hewer. Together Virginia and Leonard overlook the garden that they both cherished. It is a fitting memorial.

At the other end of the wall from the bust of Virginia is the head of Leonard, sculpted by Charlotte Hewer in 1968.
OVERLEAF Miranda, the statue bought by Leonard and Virginia, looks across the bowling terrace towards Mount Caburn.

# Timeline of Houses

| HOMES IN LONDON | | | HOMES IN THE COUNTRY | |
|---|---|---|---|---|
| | | 1880 | | |
| 22 Hyde Park Gate | 1882–1904 | | 1882–95 | Talland House, St Ives |
| | | 1890 | | |
| | | 1900 | | |
| 46 Gordon Square | 1904–06 | | | |
| 29 Fitzroy Square | 1907–11 | | | |
| 38 Brunswick Square | 1911–12 | 1910 | 1911–12 | Little Talland House, Firle |
| 13 Clifford's Inn | 1912–13 | | 1912–19 | Asheham House |
| 17 The Green, Richmond | 1914–15 | | | |
| Hogarth House, Richmond | 1915–24 | | | |
| | | 1920 | 1919–41 | Monk's House, Rodmell |
| 52 Tavistock Square | 1924–39 | | | |
| | | 1930 | | |
| 37 Mecklenburgh Square | 1939–40 | 1940 | | |

# Timeline of Books

## Works by Virginia Woolf

The *Voyage Out* (March 1915)
*Two Stories* (July 1917)
*Kew Gardens* (May 1919)
*Night and Day* (October 1919)
*Monday or Tuesday* (April 1921)
*Jacob's Room* (October 1922)
*The Common Reader* (April 1925)
*Mrs. Dalloway* (May 1925)
*To the Lighthouse* (May 1927)
*Orlando* (October 1928)
*A Room of One's Own* (October 1929)
*The Waves* (October 1931)
*The Common Reader: Second Series* (October 1932)
*Flush* (October 1933)
*The Years* (March 1937]
*Three Guineas* (June 1938)
*Roger Fry* (July 1940)
*Between the Acts* (July 1941)

## Diaries and Letters

*The Diary Of Virginia Woolf* - 5 vols (1977–1983, ed. Anne Olivier Bell)
*The Letters of Virginia Woolf* - 6 vols ( 1975–1980, ed. Nigel Nicolson)

# Bibliography

Barrett, Frank, *Treasured Island: A Book-lover's Tour of Britain* (AA Publishing, 2015)
Bartholomew, Jim, *Guide to Rodmell* (1985)
Bell, Alan, (ed) *Sir Leslie Stephen's Mausoleum Book* (Clarendon Press, 1977)
Bell, Anne Olivier, *Asheham Diary* (Charleston Magazine 9, 1994)
– (ed) *The Diary of Virginia Woolf* 5 vols (Hogarth Press, 1979–1985)
– *Editing Virginia Woolf's Diary* (The Bloomsbury Workshop, 1990)
Bell, Quentin, *Virginia Woolf: A Biography* 2 vols (Hogarth Press, 1972)
Bell, Vanessa, *Notes on Virginia's Childhood: A Memoir* (Frank Hallman, 1974)
– *Sketches in Pen and Ink* (Hogarth Press, 1997)
Bicknell, John, (ed) *Selected Letters of Leslie Stephen*, 2 vols (Macmillan, 1996, 1997)
Curtis, Vanessa, *The Hidden Houses of Virginia Woolf and Vanessa Bell* (Robert Hale, 2005)
Davies, Margaret Llewelyn, *Life As We Have Known It: by Co-operative Working Women*; introduction by Virginia Woolf (Hogarth Press, 1931)
Dell, Marion, *Peering Through the Escallonia: Virginia Woolf, Talland House and St Ives* (Cecil Woolf, 1999)
Dell, Marion, and Whybrow, Marion, *Virginia Woolf & Vanessa Bell: Remembering St Ives* (Tabb House, 2004)
Dunn, Jane, *A Very Close Conspiracy: Vanessa Bell and Virginia Woolf* (Cape, 1990)
Easdale, Gladys, *Middle Age 1885–1932* (Constable, 1935)
Gardner, Diana, *The Rodmell Papers: Reminiscences of Virginia and Leonard Woolf by a Sussex Neighbour* (Cecil Woolf, 2008)
Garnett, Angelica, *Deceived with Kindness: A Bloomsbury Childhood* (Chatto & Windus, 1984)
Glendinning, Victoria, *Leonard Woolf* (Simon and Schuster, 2006)
Hancock, Nuala, *Charleston and Monk's House: The Intimate House Museums of Virginia Woolf and Vanessa Bell* (Edinburgh University Press, 2012)
Hansen, Carol, *The Life and Death of Asham: Leonard and Virginia's Haunted House* (Cecil Woolf, 2000)
Hill-Miller, Katherine, *From The Lighthouse to Monk's House: A Guide to Virginia Woolf's Literary Landscapes* (Duckworth, 2001)
Humm, Maggie, *Snapshots of Bloomsbury* (Tate Publishing, 2006)
Kennedy, Richard, *A Boy at the Hogarth Press* (Heinemann, 1972)
Leaska, Mitchell, (ed) *A Passionate Apprentice: The Early Journals of Virginia Woolf (1897–1909)* (Hogarth Press, 1990)
Lee, Hermione, *Virginia Woolf* (Chatto & Windus, 1996)
Lehmann, John, *Thrown to the Woolfs* (Weidenfeld and Nicolson, 1978)
– *The Whispering Gallery* (Longmans, 1955)
Light, Alison, *Mrs Woolf and the Servants* (Fig Tree, 2007)
Maclear, Kyo, (illustrated by Isabelle Arsenault) *Virginia Wolf* (Book Island, 2017)
McQueeney, Maire, (ed) *Virginia Woolf's Rodmell* (Rodmell Village Press, 1991)
Maitland, Frederic, *The Life and Letters of Leslie Stephen* (Duckworth, 1906)

# BIBLIOGRAPHY

Nicolson, Nigel, (ed) *The Letters of Virginia Woolf* 6 vols (Hogarth Press, 1975–1980)
Noble, Joan Russell, (ed) *Recollections of Virginia Woolf* (Penguin, 1975)
Pearce, Brian Louis, *Virginia Woolf and the Bloomsbury Group in Twickenham* (Twickenham Local History Society, 2007)
Reed, Christopher, *Bloomsbury Rooms* (Yale University Press, 2004)
– *Roger Fry's Durbins: A House and its Meanings* (Cecil Woolf, 1999)
Schulkind, Jeanne, (ed) *Moments of Being* (Chatto & Windus for Sussex University Press, 1976)
Shone, Richard, *Asheham House, an Outline History* (*Charleston Magazine* 9, 1994)
Singleton, Julie, *A History of Monk's House and Village of Rodmell* (Cecil Woolf, 2008)
Spalding, Frances, *Virginia Woolf: Art, Life and Vision* (National Portrait Gallery, 2014)
Spater, George and Parsons, Ian, *A Marriage of True Minds* (Hogarth Press, 1977)
Spotts, Frederic, (ed) *Letters of Leonard Woolf* (Bloomsbury, 1990)
Whybrow, Marion, *Virginia Woolf & Vanessa Bell: A Childhood in St Ives* (Halsgrove, 2014)
Wilson, Jean Moorcroft, *Leonard Woolf: Pivot or Outsider of Bloomsbury* (Cecil Woolf, 1994)
– *Virginia Woolf, Life and London: a biography of place* (Cecil Woolf, 1987)
Woolf, Cecil, *The Other Boy at the Hogarth Press* (Cecil Woolf, 2017)
Woolf, Leonard, *Beginning Again* (Hogarth Press, 1964)
– *Downhill All the Way* (Hogarth Press, 1967)
– *The Journey Not the Arrival Matters* (Hogarth Press, 1969)
Wright, Sarah Bird, *Staying at Monk's House: Echoes of the Woolfs* (Cecil Woolf, 1995)
Zoob, Caroline, *Virginia Woolf's Garden* (Jacqui Small, 2013)

## USEFUL WEBLINKS

– www.nationaltrust.org.uk/monks-house
– www.virginiawoolfsociety.org.uk. The Virginia Woolf Bulletin is produced three times a year
– www.bloggingwoolf.wordpress.com
– www.smith.edu/libraries/libs/rarebook/exhibitions/stephen/
– www.roh.org.uk/news/max-richter-on-how-he-composed-the-score-for-woolf-works
– www.roh.org.uk/news/he-likes-you-explore-the-characters-and-the-movement-to-the-maximum-artists-of-the-royal-ballet-on-working-with-mcgregor

# Index

## A
Adam, Robert 55, 60, 187
*After the Deluge* 118
Albee, Edward 181
Alfriston 101
*Alpine Journal* 11
Anrep, Boris 185
Arnold-Forster, Will 88
Asheham 7, 67, 70, 73, 77, 78, 79, 84, 87, *98*, 99–110, 143, 146, 148, 149, 173, 177, 188–9, 198

## B
Badger Inn *61*, 62
Bagnold, Enid 30
Barker, Marjorie 180
Bartholomew, Marie 153, 174, 176, 195
Bartholomew, Percy 146, 153, 155, 158, 174, 176, 195
Bartholomew, Rose 146
Bedford Estates 114, 136, 140
Bedford Square 62, 63, 67
*Beginning Again* 84, 190
'Being Despised' 136
Bell, Angelica 61, 106, 138, 145, *154*, *170*
Bell, Anne Olivier 180, 199
Bell, Clive 7, 43, 45, 53, 55, 60, 65, 66, 73, 74, 102, 106, 110, 120, 124, *154*
Bell, Julian 59, 60, 106, *106*, 138, 140, 156, 169
Bell, Julian (Quentin's son) 173
Bell, Quentin 73, 106, *106*, 123, 173, 180
Bell, Vanessa (*née* Stephen) 9, 10, 12, *14*, 24, *25*, 31, 34, 35, 36, 38, 40, 42, 43, 45, 46, 48, 53, 54, 55, 59, 60–1, 65, 66, 67, 73, 77, 78, 79, 93, 101, 102, 103, 104, 105–6, 107, 108, 109, 110, 116, 124, *125*, 134, 138, 140, 141, 143, *154*, 156, 158, 170, 175, 183, 185, 186
and interior design 49, 85, 100, 120, 151–3, 192
*Between the Acts* (originally *Pointz Hall*) 140, 144, 166, 173–4, 176, 179, 190
Birkbeck College 55, 187
Blo' Norton Hall 54
Bloomsbury 7, 34, 45–70, 74, 81, 114, 115, 138, 140, 185, 186
Bloomsbury Group 52, 53, 63, 115, 120, 186
Bogarde, Dirk 167
Bolitho, Mr 15
Bowen, Elizabeth 122, 138, 174, 176
Boxall, Nellie 87, 90, 103, 104, 117, 126, 136, 146, 149, 150, 161
*Boy at the Hogarth Press, A* 15
Brighton 29, 41, 42, 177
British Museum 81, 95, 113
Brooke, Rupert 24, 101
Browning, Elizabeth Barrett 135
Browning, Robert 49
Brunswick Square 67, 140
38 Brunswick Square 70, 74, 77, 78, 81, 198
Burne-Jones, Edward 22
Burnham Wood 42, 47, *47*

## C
Cambridge 43, 48, 49, 51, 52, 53, 62, 69, 75, 134, 143, 181
Cameron, Julia Margaret 24, 30, *32*, 49, 120, 138
Campbell, Duncan 181
Carlyle, Thomas 30, 41, 115
Case, Janet 36, 63, 79, 146
Cassis 134, 138
Ceylon 48, 65, 67, 69, 81, 118
Charleston 93, *104–5*, 105, 106, 138, 143, 158, 167, 170
Chart, Maud (housemaid) 57, 69, 100
Chatto & Windus 185, 189–90
Christie, Agatha 146, 149
Churchill, Winston 30, 63
Clifford's Inn 74, 75, *75*, 76, 77, 78, 81, 97, 102, 125, 179, 198
Colefax, Lady Sybil 122, *122*
Coleridge, Samuel Taylor 74
*Common Reader, The* 123, 128, 149
Connolly, Cyril 137
*Cornhill Magazine, The* 11, 65, 127
Cornwall 9–27, 37, 54, 61, 67, 79, 83, 89, 118, 146
Cox, Katherine (Ka) 76, 78, 79, 88, 143
Cubitt, Thomas 114–5, *115*

## D
Dalingridge Place *71*, 78
Dalloway, Clarissa 30, 34, 113, 125
Darwin, Charles 49
Davidson, Angus 118
Davies, Margaret Llewelyn 63, 77, 82, 83, 163
Dean, Christopher 146
*Deceived with Kindness* 61
Dedman, Mrs 146
Dedman, William 146
Dickens, Charles 76, 113, 115, 135
Dickinson, Violet 42, 43, 45, 47, *48*, 49, 51, 54, 56, 57, 59, 65, 67, 69, 78, 91, 100, 106, 124
*Dictionary of National Biography* 11, 30
Disraeli, Benjamin 30
Dow, Florence Millie 27
Dow, Thomas Millie 21, 27

# INDEX

*Downhill All The Way* 174
Dreadnought Hoax 63, *64*, 173
Duckworth, George 12, 23, 24, 38, 43, 45, 46, 65, 70, 73, 78
Duckworth, Gerald 12, 23, 24, 45, 46, 77
Duckworth, Julia
   *see* Stephen, Julia
Duckworth, Stella 12, 22, 24, 38, *39*, 40, 42, 47, 83
Duckworth (publisher) 77, 118
Durbins 87, 103

## E
Easdale, Gladys 165
Eliot, T.S. 92, *94*
Eliot, Vivienne *94*
Everest, Louie 161, *161*, 176, 179, 192

## F
Fabian Society, 77, 80, 86, 103
*Far from the Madding Crowd* 127
Farrell, Sophie (cook) 23, 40, 56, 57, *57*, 69, 100, 198
Firle 67, 100, 101, 107
First World War 47, 84, 87, 103
Fisher, Jo 40
Fisher, Mary 42, 73
Fitzroy Square 55, *60*, 63, 85, 187
   29 Fitzroy Square 55, 56, *58*, 187, 198
*Flush* 135, 199
Forster, E.M. 7, 43, 110, 120, 127, 135, 143, 163
*Freshwater* 38, 138
Freud, Sigmund 120
Fritham 42
Fry, Margery 136, 139
Fry, Roger 73, 77, 85, 86, 87, 103, 120, 139

## G
Gardner, Diana 165
Garnett, Angelica
   *see* Bell, Angelica
Garnett, David 106, 135
Garsington Manor 63, 66, *68*
Gladstone, William 30
Giggleswick 49
Godrevy Lighthouse *15*, 16, 17, *18–19*, 20, 23, 26, 187
*Good Housekeeping* 41
Gordon Square 46, 50, 53, 55, 57, 70, 96, 114, 117, 138, 140
   46 Gordon Square *44*, 45, 46, 49, *51*, 53, 54, 55, 59, 73, 88, 162, 186, 187, 198
Grant, Duncan 63, 69, 73, 77, 81, 85, 106, 110, 116, 140, 151, 153
Grant, Ethel 153
*Granta* 135
Graves, Robert 120
'Great Men's Houses' 41
Great Western Railway 15, 23
Greece 54, 138, 169
17 The Green, Richmond 79, *80*, 198
*Guardian, The* (Anglican journal) 49, 53, 65

## H
Hamill, Frances 180
Hampstead 36
Hanson, Joshua Flesher 29, 30
Hardy, Thomas 127
Haskins, Mabel 136
'Haunted House, A' 99
'Haworth, November 1904' 49, 53
Hepworth, Barbara 12
Herbert, Lady Margaret 46
Herschel, William 49
Heron, Patrick 13
Hewer, Charlotte 195

Highgate Cemetery 40
Hill, Octavia 22
Hills, Jack 40, 46, 83
Hogarth House 79, 81, 82, *82*, 83, 84, 88, 96, 114, 146, 187–8, 198
*Hogarth Living Poets* 117
Hogarth Press 7, 15, 85, 90–5, 107, 114, 116–118, 120, 121, 140, 189–90
   printing press 89, 90, *90*, 91, 92, 121
   publications
   *see* individual titles
Holford 73
Holtby, Winifred 118, 135, 181
Hope, Lottie 87, 103, 117
*Hours, The see Mrs Dalloway*
*Hours, The* (film) 183
Howells, W.D. 53
Hudson, Nan 129
Hunt, William Holman 30
Hyde Park Gate 29, 30, 33
   13 Hyde Park Gate
   *see* 22 Hyde Park Gate
   22 Hyde Park Gate 11, 12, 23, 26, *28*, 29–43, *31*, 46, 49, 50, 55, 56, 135, 146, 186, 187, 198
   24 Hyde Park Gate 12, 40
*Hyde Park Gate News* 26

## I
*International Government* 87
*International Review* 86
Isle of Wight 38, 115, 138

## J
*Jacob's Room* 10, 81, 93, 113, 126, 134
Jackson, Julia *see* Stephen, Julia
James, Henry 22, 65
Joad, Marjorie 93, 118
John, Augustus 63

Johnson, Samuel 76
'Journal of Mistress Joan Martyn, The' 54
Joyce, James 92

**K**
Kennedy, George 158
Kennedy, Richard 15, 158
Kensington 11, 12, 30, 38, 46, 50, 135, 186
Kensington Gardens 29, 37, *37*, 41, 81
*Kew Gardens* 93, 107, *107*, 109
Keynes, Geoffrey 78
Keynes, John Maynard 43, 45, 63, 69, 88, 110, 120
Keynes, Lydia 88
Knills monument 24
Knole 121, *121*, 129, 130
Koteliansky, S.S. 93
Kukil, Karen 181

**L**
*Lady Chatterley's Lover* 48
Lawrence, D.H. 48, 107
Lawrence, Frieda 107
Lamb, Walter 88
Landmark Trust 171
Laughton Place 170–1
Lehmann, John 118, *119*, 159, 176
Lelant Hotel *see* Badger Inn
Lewes 67, 93, 99, 102, 107, 109, 120, 145, 146, 149, 154, 155, 156, 158, 162, 169, 174, 175, 177, 180
Lewis, Cecil Day 120
Little Holland House 30
Little Talland House 100, *101*, 107, 198
Lobb, Mr (caretaker) 17
London 9, 23, 29, 31, 45
London Library 81, 135
Lowell, James 22
Lyttelton, Kathleen 49

**M**
Macaulay, Rose 127
MacGregor, Wayne 184
Maitland, Frederic 48
Mansfield, Katherine 92, *92*, 107
*Manchester Guardian* 36, 77
Manorbier 45, 65
'Mark on the Wall, The' 91, 93
*Mausoleum Book* 30, 33
37 Mecklenburgh Square 140, 173
Melbury Road 30
Meredith, George 22
Millais, John Everett 22
Mitz the marmoset 137, *137*, 183
Monk's House 84, 93, 109, 110, 110–11, 128, 135, *142*, 143–173, *147*, *148*, *150–1*, *152*, *155*, *160*, *163*, *172*, 175, *175*, *188*, 189, 192, 193, 195, 198
Monk's House garden 153, 154, *164*, 171, 191, *193*, 195
Morley College 53
Morrell, Lady Ottoline *62*, 62, 63, 100, 122
Morris, William 34, 49, 88
Mosley, Oswald 114
*Mrs Dalloway* 30, 47, 88, 95, 113, 123, 125, 128, 149, 156, 183, 184, 185
*Moths, The see Waves, The*

**N**
*Nation, The* 95, 118
National Trust 26, 192, 193
New Forest 36, 42, 59
*New Statesman, The* 86, 118, 127
New York Public Library 180, 192
Nicholson, Ben 13
Nicolson, Benedict *133*
Nicolson, Harold 121, 129
Nicolson, Nigel *133*, 180, 192
*Night and Day* 75, 93, 113, 118, 122, 126
Nine Maidens, the 17

Norfolk 54
Norton, Charles 11, 13
Nurse Traill 51

**O**
'Old Bloomsbury' 34
Omega Workshops 85, 86, 192
*Orlando* 113, 130, 132, *132*, 134, 158, 183, 184, 185
Oxford Street 50, 82, 85, 88, 125
Ouse, River 149, 156, *177*, 195

**P**
Paignton 33
Painswick 40
*The Pargiters see The Years*
Parsons, Ian 189
Parsons, Trekkie 189, *189*, 192
Partridge, Ralph 93
Pattle sisters 30
Pater, Clara 36
Pater, Walter 36
Pembrokeshire 45
Pepys, Samuel 76
'Phyllis and Rosamund' 53
'Plague of Essays, A' 65
Plough Inn, Holford 73, 78
*Pointz Hall see Between the Acts*
*Political Quarterly* 118
Porthminster Beach 20
*Prelude* 92
Prinsep, Sarah 30
*Punch* (magazine) 40

**R**
Ramsay, James 26
Ramsay, Mrs 20
Redgrave, Mrs 30
Richmond 79, 80, 95
Richmond, Bruce 65
Richter, Max 184–5
Ritchie, Alice 189
Ritchie, Anny (*née* Thackeray) 12, 30, 33
Ritchie, Richmond 33
Rodin 45

# INDEX

Rodmell 93, 101, 109, 149, 150, 168, 169, 173, 175, 192, 195
Rodmell Horticultural Society 190–1, *190*, *191*
Rodmell Women's Institute 65, 173
*Room of One's Own, A* 134, 137, 158
Rossetti, Dante Gabriel 30
Round House, The 107, *108*, 109
Russell, Bertrand 63
Rylands, Dadie 118

## S

Sackville-West, Vita 120, 121, 128, *131*, *133*, 150, 163, 171
and *Orlando* 130
works – *Seducers in Ecuador* 120; *The Edwardians* 122
and Virginia Woolf *see* Woolf, Virginia and Vita Sackville-West
St Erth 23
St Ives 9, 12, 13, *13–14*, 20, 22, 23, 26, 27, 33, 38, 42, 59
St Ives Arts Club 20
St Ives Bay 16, 17, *20*, 26
St Ives Regatta 20
Tate Gallery 12–13
St Peter's Church, Rodmell 144, *145*
Salisbury 43
Sands, Ethel 129, 155
Savage, Dr 47, 48, 50, 66, 82
Seaford 103, 156, 177
Second World War 140, 174–5
Seton, Dr 38
Shaw, Charlotte 81
Shaw, George Bernard 55, 56, *56*, 81
Sheepshanks, Mary 53, 63
Sissinghurst Castle 122, 132, *133*
Sitwell, Edith 120
'Sketch of the Past, A' 9, 16, 26, 43
Skye 26, 138
Smith, George 11

Smith, Septimus Warren 47
Smyth, Dame Ethel 137, *137*, 166
*Son of Royal Langbrith, The* 53
Southwell Gardens 12, 30
Spanish Civil War 140
Spender, Stephen 127
Stephen, Adrian 12, *14*, 25, 26, 36, 38, 42, 45, 54, 55, 56, 59, 62, 69, 96, 102, 117, 138
Stephen, James 126
Stephen, Julia (*née* Jackson) 9, 12, *14*, 17, 20, *22*, 22, 24, 26, 30, *32*, 33, 34, *35*, 35, 36, 37, 38, 43
Stephen, Karin 96, 117
Stephen, Laura 12, 33, 46
Stephen, Leslie 9, 11, 12, 13, 15, 16, 17, 20, *22*, 22, 24, 29, 30, 31, 33, 35, 36, 37, 38, 40, *41*, 41, 43, 45, 48, 127
Stephen, Minny (née Thackeray) 30, 33
Stephen, Thoby 9, 12, *14*, 36, 42, 43, 45, 48, 49, *52*, 53, 54, 55, 59, 134
Stephen, Vanessa *see* Bell, Vanessa
Stephen, Virginia *see* Woolf, Virginia
Strachey, Lytton 42, 43, 53, 55, 65, 66, *66*, 74, 79, 91, 134, 139, 173
Studland 67
Suffield House 95, 146, 187–8
Surrey 43, 81
Sussex 67, 99, 100, 110, 158, 162, *166*, 167, *167*, 170, 189, 192
Sydney-Turner, Saxon 53, 73, 96

## T

Talland House 9, *9*, 10, 11, 12, 13, *14*, 15, 16, *16*, 17, 20, 21, 22, *22*, 24, 25, 26, 27, 29, 54, 79, 186–7, 198
Tavistock Square *116*, 126, 140

52 Tavistock Square 84, 96, 97, 113, 116, 175, 186, 198
Tennyson, Alfred 30, 49, 138
Terry, Ellen 138
Thackeray, Anny 12, 30
Thackeray, Minny (Harriet) 11
Thackeray, William Makepeace 11, 30
Thomas, Jean 67
Thomsett, Annie 161, 173
'Three Guineas' 136
'Three Jews, The' 91
*Times Literary Supplement* 65, 123
*To the Lighthouse* 10, 15, 16, 20, 26, 36, 127, 130, 156, 162, 182
Todd, Dorothy 123
Tomlin, Stephen 179, 185, 195
Tregenna Castle Estate 15
Tregenna Castle Hotel 22
Trencrom Hill 26, *27*, 62
*Two Stories* 90, 91

## U

University College London 53, 55, 69

## V

Vaughan, Emma 42, 91
Vaughan, Madge 49, 54, 65
Vaughan, Will 49
Verrall, Jacob 146
24 Victoria Square 179
*Village in the Jungle, The* 69
*Virginia Woolf: A Biography* 180
*Virginia Woolf: A Critical Memoir* 180–81
Virginia Woolf Society (UK) 123, 182, 185, 186
*Voyage Out, The* 54, 65, 66, 67, 75, 77, 83, 93, 118, 125, 136

## W

Waddesdon 138
Wallis, Alfred 13
Watts, George Frederic 22

Watts, Isaac 42
*Waves, The* 10, 132, *134*, 134, 183, 184, 190
Webb, Beatrice and Sidney 77, 80, 81, 87, *103*
Wellesley, Dorothy 117
West, Rebecca 174
Whitbread, Hugh 88
*Who's Afraid of Virginia Woolf?* 181
Wilberforce, Octavia 176
Wimbledon 82
Women's Co-operative Guild 77, 83, 86, 88, 102
Woolf, Cecil 7, 118, 120, 138, 160
Woolf, Leonard 6, 7, 38, 43, 48, 63, 67, 69, *71*, 76, 77, 78, 79, 80, 81, 82, 83, 91, 95, 96, 101, 102, 103, 105, 114, 116, 117, 120, 123, 124, 126, 127, 130, 132, 134, 136, 137, 138, *141*, 146, 148, 150, 151, 159, 160, 162, 163, 166, 167, 168, 169, 173, 188, 189, *194*
  career 86–7, 90, 118, 136, 190
  death of 192–3
  driving 156–8
  finances 128–9
  gardening and gardens 102, 104, 143, 146, 153–5, 164, *164*, 171, 174, 189, 191, *193*, 195
  health 124, 156
  Hogarth Press
    *see* Hogarth Press
  house-hunting 88, 106–10, 140, 170–1
  importance of houses 84, 99, 130, 144, 170
  Labour Party 118, 136
  love of animals 6, 120, 139, *141*
  marriage to Virginia 66, 70, 73, 74
  Virginia's death 176–7, 179
  Virginia's diaries 179–80
  works *see individual titles*
Woolf, Philip 138,
Woolf, Virginia (*née* Stephen) 6, 7, *8, 14,* 22, *25,* 30, 31, 33, 34, 35, *35,* 36, 39, 40, 41, *41,* 43, *48,* 49, 50, 51, 59, 62, 63, 64, *64,* 66, *66,* 67, 68, 69, *71, 73,* 77, 86, *89, 94,* 101, *112, 119, 123, 131, 133, 137,* 139, *154, 159, 178, 187*
  birth of Virginia 9, 11, 12, 29
  breakdowns and illness 38, 47–8, 66, 70, 77–9, 83, 84, 102, 123–4, 136, 144, 156, 176
  childhood 16, 20, 23, 24, 26, 37
  cooking 76, 79, 81, 87, 100, 103, 104, 162
  death of 177, 179
  domesticity 75, 85, 87, 136, 146, 155–6
  driving *see* Woolf, Leonard and driving
  finances 128–9, 149, 155
  gardening 38, 77, 154–5
  Hogarth Press 85, 90–3, 117, 118, 120, 121–2
  holidays 45, 54, 66, 79, 138, 169
  homes 88, 99, 101, 110, 114, 116, 117, 143, 144, 148, 149, 150–3, 158–165, 169, 192–3
  house-hunting 46, 55–7, 81, 95–7, 106–10, 140, 169–71
  legacy of 179–95
  marriage to Leonard 70, 73, 74, 80, 129, 130, 171–3
  needlework 153, 162
  relationship with Vanessa 34–5, 42, 59, 61, 100, 104, 140
  social life 65, 81, 101, 122–3, 127, 137, 165, 173, 174, 176
  suicide 176–7
  and Vita Sackville-West 120–1, 129–30, 132
  walking 50, 124–6, 154, 167
  works *see individual titles*
  writing 42, 53, 60, 65, 69, 77, 113, 130, 132, 134–6, 139–40, 166, 168, 174, 184
*Woolf Works* 183, *183*
*Writer's Diary, A* 180

# Y
Ye Olde Cock Tavern 76, *76*
*Years, The* 34, 37, 50, 113, 135, 136, 165, 190

# Acknowledgments

I have followed in the footsteps of Virginia Woolf for some time, looking at her homes before and after marriage to Leonard and reading their strong views on the importance of houses in one's life. And it greatly pleases me that Cecil Woolf, Leonard's nephew (and publisher of a wealth of information on aspects of Bloomsbury), agreed to write the Foreword.

I'd like to thank Andrew Dunn for early encouragement of my interest and, most especially, publisher Jo Christian of Pimpernel Press, who followed the progress of my research with enthusiasm. I very much appreciate the contribution made by those who have also worked on the book: designer Becky Clarke, editor Anna Sanderson, proofreader Vanessa Bird and, in particular, picture editor Sue Gladstone, whose expertise led to a pleasurable partnership.

I want to thank the Society of Authors as the Literary Representative of the Estate of Virginia Woolf, and The University of Sussex and The Society of Authors as the Literary Representative of the Estate of Leonard Woolf – in particular Sarah Baxter and Sarah Burton for their advice – and also Henrietta Garnett for allowing us to include photographs from the Estate of Vanessa Bell held by the Victoria University Library, Toronto.

Karen Kukil, Associate Curator of Special Collections at Smith College and curator of the online exhibition of Leslie Stephen's Photograph Album, has from the beginning of my research been supportive and generous. Thanks to Professor Jane de Gay and Hayley Cook of Leeds Trinity University, I attended the 2016 International Conference on Virginia Woolf and Heritage, which gave me additional insight; Suzanne Raitt and Allison Adler Kroll kindly sent papers from sessions I could not attend.

I am grateful to Allison Pritchard, curator of Monk's House, who helpfully passed on the room notes; Marie Bartholomew, daughter of Leonard's gardener; and Christine Isitt, who sent me notes about the beginnings of the Rodmell Horticultural Society.

I'd like to thank Russell Long of the Environment Agency for solving a puzzle about the River Ouse. In Richmond, George Drower and Peter Fullager supplied useful material and Lee Pascal gave me interesting news about Hogarth House that led me to Hannah Durden and Jeremy Richardson of Berwick Hill Properties, which has painstakingly restored Hogarth House: Hannah invited me to see it as it is now. Others who contributed have been Barry Edwards, who gave me a collection of books on Virginia Woolf; David Fenton, with his knowledge of St Ives; and Duncan Campbell, who provided me with a story about the ubiquity of Virginia Woolf's works among prisoners.

Most of all, I want to express my appreciation of daughters Judith and Anna for their encouragement – and assistance when requested – and of Michael Shipman who accompanied me to all the places associated with the Woolfs, provided many of the photographs and kept me informed of the almost daily appearances of Virginia Woolf in the media.

# Picture Credits

The Publishers have made every effort to contact holders of copyright works. Any copyright holders we have been unable to reach are invited to contact the Publishers so that a full acknowledgment may be given in subsequent editions. For permission to reproduce the images below, the Publishers would like to thank the following:

Alamy Stock Photo: 48 & 103 (Granger Historical Picture Archive), 104/105 (Mike Coombes), 147, 148, 150, 151, 164, 172, 175, 178, 193, 194 & 196/7 (The National Trust Photo Library), 152 & 155 (Albert Knapp), 188 (Bernard Philpot)
Courtesy of Laury Dizengremel and Aurora Metro: 187
Thomas Erskine: 82
©CSG CIC Glasgow Museums Collection: 20/21
Historic Newspapers: 64
Houghton Library, Harvard University: 6 MS Thr 561 (49); 25( above) MS Thr 564 (50); 25 (below) MS Thr 557 (88); 39 MS Thr 557 (160); 41 MS Thr 557 (180); 52 MS Thr 557 (184); 57 MS Thr 561 (60); 66 MS Thr 560 (138); 68 MS Thr 564 (57); 83 MS Thr 559 (26); 89 MS Thr 559 (21); 94 MS Thr 560 (87); 98 MS Thr 557 (191); 106 MS Thr 562 (161); 112 MS Thr 564 (73); 116 (MS Thr 564 (152, sequence 2); 117 MS Thr 561 (50); 119 MS Thr 560 (40); 122 MS Thr 560 (19); 131 MS Thr 560 (100); 133 MS Thr 562 (41); 137 MS Thr 560 (145); 139 MS Thr 562 (126); 142 MS Thr 564 (147, sequence 5); 144 MS Thr 560 (158); 145 MS Thr 564 (147, sequence 3); 154 MS Thr 560 (185); 157 MS Thr 560 (11); 159 MS Thr 564 (244, sequence 2); 160 MS Thr 564 (147, sequence 4); 161 MS Thr 562 (99); 163 MS Thr 562 (189); 170 MS Thr 562 (111); 189 MS Thr 561 (104)
©National Portrait Gallery: 72, 141
National River Agency: 177
NYPL digital collections: 47
Private Collection: 184
By kind permission of the Richmond Borough Art Collection, Orleans House Gallery: 80
Alex Sanderson (Instagram@palex.sanderson): 15
Michael Shipman: 4, 12/13, 16, 17, 18/19, 27, 28, 31, 44, 51, 56 (right), 58, 60, 61, 75, 76, 85, 90, 101, 108, 109, 110/11, 115, 123, 126, 166, 167, 186, 190, 191
Shutterstock: 182, 183
Courtesy of Smith College, Special Collections: 8, 14 above, 14 below, 22, 35, 71, 107
Victoria University Library, Toronto: 132
Victoria University Library, Toronto ©Estate of Vanessa Bell, courtesy of Henrietta Garnett: 10, 125, 134
Wikimedia Commons: 2, 32, 37, 56 (left), 62, 86 (cc-by-sa-3.0), 92 (cc-by-sa-2.0), 121